William Carew Hazlitt

**A hundred merry tales:**

The earliest English jest-book

William Carew Hazlitt

**A hundred merry tales:**
*The earliest English jest-book*

ISBN/EAN: 9783337715038

Printed in Europe, USA, Canada, Australia, Japan

Cover: Foto ©ninafisch / pixelio.de

More available books at **www.hansebooks.com**

# A Hundred Merry Tales:

*THE EARLIEST ENGLISH JEST-BOOK.*

NOW FIRST REPRODUCED IN PHOTO-LITHOGRAPHY

FROM THE UNIQUE COPY

OF 1526

IN THE ROYAL LIBRARY AT GÖTTINGEN.

*WITH AN INTRODUCTION, NOTES, AND*

*GLOSSARIAL INDEX*

BY

W. CAREW HAZLITT.

LONDON :

*J. W. JARVIS & SON,*

2S, *KING WILLIAM STREET, STRAND.*

1887.

# EDITOR'S PREFACE.

THERE may be some, who will attach value and interest to the singular old volume, now first reproduced in exact imitation of the original, on account of the casual mention of it by Shakespear in one of his plays ; but I hope and think that many more will welcome its appearance on another and higher ground, and will become of opinion that, where a solitary copy of such a relic as the earliest jest-book in the national tongue of England is only to be found in a foreign repository, and is liable to destruction at any moment, the survival, not of its mere substance alone, but of its very identity, in the shape of a facsimile, is one of those minor duties, which we owe to succeeding generations.

In the good former days, a gentleman who did his friends and the public the favour of reprinting a curious old book, was regarded as a sort of benefactor by a few who knew a little about the matter, and by the greater number, who knew nothing, he was considered a person of elegant tastes and of liberal disposition ; for he usually engaged in the speculation on his own responsibility. The case is now altogether altered, and any one who proposes to give to the world a new edition of an old book or tract, is in peril of being received as a Frenchman receives the news of his third child, unless he can make out a pretty strong plea for his proceeding. He must bring his justification in his hand. The burden of proof is upon him.

In the present instance, the enterprise on which the Editor has entered, is one which seems, at first sight, not to be without its element of superfluity, for in 1866 the book which is now in question was brought out under the care of Dr. Herman Oesterley from the same copy which I employ.[1] But I believe that I hold, notwithstanding, a very fair brief for my clients ; for it was considered that the *Hundred Merry Tales* had so many claims to special consideration :—as being the most ancient book of its kind in the English language ; as existing only in a complete state in a single copy preserved in a Continental library ; and as the volume, out of which, in *Much Ado about Nothing*, 1600, Beatrice tells us she had been charged with stealing all her good wit. So the great poet makes her say, at least ; but the accusation was, so far as we can judge, an unfair one, and between the wit of the book and that of the lady there is little in common.

When the present editor republished the work as one of a collection more than twenty years ago, he had access only to the text of Singer ; he had, at a later period, an opportunity of collating it with the original, at that time in the possession of Mr. Halliwell-Phillipps ; but the copy, as it is tolerably well-known, had been made up from an assortment of mutilated leaves, and presented a considerable number of *lacunæ*, including entire tales, so that, until the Göttingen copy occurred, we had in fact no means of studying this, in every sense, unique publication in its full integrity.

But the Göttingen copy and that included in *Old English Jest Books*, 1864, belonged to different impressions, and the former contains matter, which never formed part of the latter. Some items were left out to make room for others which were deemed fresher and more attractive ; and the entire arrangement was altered. The edition of 1526 includes four tales, which are not in that without date, but omits three found in the latter.

The articles special to the present issue are the second,

---

[1] Shakespeare's Jest Book. A Hundred Mery Talys, from the only perfect copy known. Edited, with Introduction and Notes, by Dr. Herman Oesterley, London, 1866, 12mo, pp. 160 + XX.

ninth, ninety-first, and ninety-eighth stories. It does not give Numbers 97, 99, and 100 of the other issue, which I annex in an Appendix, all being unhappily defective. There appears more than one error in the numeration of the calendar or table; for there is no Number 42 in it, although a title, which should have been so registered, intervenes between 41 and 43 ; while, again, there is no 98 either in the Table or the text. These irregularities are of course of perpetual occurrence in the literary and typographical work of the period.

The Göttingen copy of 1526 consists of twenty-eight leaves in small folio, precisely answering to the present reproduction. It is stated by Dr. Oesterley that, according to an entry in the books of the Library, the volume was purchased in December, 1767, at an auction in Lüneburg, but that no clue could be discovered to its antecedents.

Dr. Oesterley puts forward a somewhat elaborate argument in favour of the priority of the impression first edited by himself in 1866, over the undated copy brought to light by Conybeare, and printed by Singer[1] and the present writer.[2] I shall subjoin what the learned gentleman advances :—

" The question, which of the two copies recovered up to the present moment is the original and older edition (and there is very little hope of ever discovering a third copy), will be very difficult to prove to an absolute certainty. By the want of any authentic indication, the inquiry is thrown back on a mere circumstantial proof ; but I think the reasons to be given hereafter will be strong enough to produce a firm conviction of the priority of our original.

The first argument in favour of the edition of 1526 is founded on the selection and disposition of the tales. When a reprint of a collection of a hundred tales like the one in question is being prepared, and the removing of four stories seems desirable, it is unlikely enough, that the three or four last pieces should be cast off; but it is much more unlikely that the number required to complete a hundred should be inserted in entirely chance places. This, however, would have been the case in the Nos. 2, 7, 91 and 98 of our edition, if it had been a revision of the undated copy. On the other hand, it is quite natural simply to throw out the tales considered as unserviceable (which, as before mentioned, would hardly be placed together, but be scattered throughout the work), and to subjoin the additions at the end. This has been the case, if the undated edition is the result of a revision : Nos. 2, 7, 91 and 98

---

[1] Shakespeare Jest Book, 1814, 12mo.

[2] Shakespeare Jest Books, 1864, 12mo, 3 vols.

of the original edition have been suppressed, and in their stead Nos. 97 to 100 of the later impression are added. I must say, that this mode of revision, in a work where the disposition of the matter is entirely arbitrary, seems to me more natural than even putting the new stories in the place of the old ones. The substance of the tales in discussion can be of no moment for the question, for indeed the one is about as insipid as the other, and moreover, the taste of our ancestors in regard to jests and popular tales was so very different from ours, that it is next to impossible at present to decide which of them might be considered more palatable to the public at that time.

The transposition of a single tale to another place[1] can, of course, be no conclusive argument either for one view or the other, whereas the want of the morals in the undated copy is of consequence, if it really be found in the original and not be produced by a defect, which is not quite evident in Mr. Hazlitt's reprint. As our copy contains twenty-eight leaves and the undated one only twenty-four, therefore the arrangement of the type in each must have been quite different; the absence of these morals might have arisen from a desire of saving space, and thus furnish a new evidence for the priority of the dated edition.

The variations in the table favour my opinion in an equal manner. Wherever any essential differences occur in the headings, they are equal to as many emendations in the undated copy,[2] and these improvements evidently bear witness to the later appearance of the revised edition; the more, as there is no trace of a third edition earlier than both, of which the undated copy might possibly be a revised impression, ours being only a later and unrevised reprint.

This might, indeed, have been the case for the alterations of the text; but under the circumstances it is too improbable to be advanced as an objection, and I may fairly put it out of the question. Among the very large quantity of variations in the text, there are, of course, many entirely irrelevant in the decision of the question, as they cannot be considered as improvements. The greater part, nevertheless, proves that the undated edition is the product of a revision. In the first place the misprints are important. The typographical errors of our edition, about fifty or sixty, have all been corrected in Mr. Hazlitt's original, in which, however, there are about twenty new misprints. The most remarkable of these is p. 35, l. 13, of Mr. Hazlitt's reprint, where, evidently from the repetition of the words "tyed fast by the leggys" in three consecutive lines (at the top of fol. vi verso of our original), more than a line of our text has been omitted, the passage ending with the first repetition of those words being left out. As it would be impossible to enumerate all the passages which go to prove my proposition, I mention only some of the most striking instances. Fol. 1 verso, l. 39, the words "his neck," accidently omitted in ours, are supplied in Mr. Hazlitt's edition; fol. 2 verso, l. 10, "for that that"—Hazl. "because;" fol. 10, l. 38,

---

[1] No. 43 to No. 32 of the undated edition.

[2] See the headings of Nos. 1 to 6, 44 and 66.

" by vyolence "—Hazl. " of the house ; " fol. 11 verso, l. 16, " thy "—Hazl. " your ; " fol. 14, l. 27, " up through "—Hazl. " throughe it," &c. ; but especially fol. 21, l. 3 and 4, a very corrupt passage of our text has been corrected in Mr. Hazlitt's edition, p. 102, l. 8 ; fol. 23, l. 2, the words "sayde in sporte" are omitted, but have been inserted in the undated copy.

On the other hand, I feel obliged to mention that a few of the variations in the undated copy cannot well be considered as corrections from our text, but rather seem to indicate the reverse ;[1] this, however, is easily enough accounted for by the fact that alterations are not always improvements : indeed, in one instance,[2] the very corruption of the text proves its being a revised edition.

The orthography in both editions is too varied and unsettled to be of any moment for our question, although the frequent use of written numbers in the undated copy instead of the simple cypher, and perhaps the employing of the word "pence " for our abbreviation d. seem to strengthen my argument. On the whole, all the orthography proves is that only a few years elapsed between the appearance of the two editions.

These are the arguments I have to present ; although each taken singly may not be considered conclusive, the whole will form as unexceptionable a proof of the priority of our edition as can be expected, and this proof is the more cogent, as there is nothing worth mentioning to be offered in favour of the other edition."

Yet to any one who is conversant with the lax and capricious manner in which editorial functions were formerly discharged, even the strong points adduced by Dr. Oesterley will scarcely seem conclusive ; and as a matter of fact the question is of no special relevance. It is of greater moment that the means exist for laying before the student a complete text, as it were, of both books, with the exception of the deficiency in the concluding tales in what the doctor holds to have been the second impression.

A much more interesting and more vital consideration is the literary history of the work ; and I do not recollect that any suggestion in furtherance or elucidation of this point has ever been submitted.

There is the excellent authority of Gabriel Harvey, the friend and fellow-collegian of Spenser, for believing that some of the epigrams of John Heywood were " conceits and devices of

---

[1] F. c. fol. 12, l. 34 ; fol. 12 verso, l. 27 ; fol. 16 verso, l. 23 ; fol. 20, l. 21, &c.

[2] Fol. 20 verso, l. 9 ; see the notes.

pleasant Sir Thomas More;" in his copy of Speght's Chaucer, Harvey, a rare annotator of his books, made a memorandum to such an effect; and, although he was not a contemporary of More, he was so of Heywood. This authoritative statement seems to possess the virtue of establishing More and Heywood on a footing of intimacy; and if we had not had such a piece of evidence, the congenial dispositions of the two men, and the connection of both with the court, might have combined to render such an intercourse and friendship on their parts alike probable and natural. Harvey explicitly declares that Heywood was under obligations to More for hints and notions, which he developed in his dramatic and poetical compositions; and many a droll anecdote must have been exchanged in the course of time between these two kindred spirits, and many a quip and joke, which had their outlet in some interlude or epigram, were doubtless indebted for their germs to a merry-making at Chelsea, Greenwich, Hampton Court, or elsewhere.

The relationship between More and the Rastells, of whom one was the printer of both issues of the *Hundred Merry Tales*, is next to be received into account; but the press of John Rastell was likewise employed in the production of all the earliest editions of the works of Heywood, as that of his brother William was of nearly all those of More. The pleasantries and outlines of plots, too, perhaps, were communicated to Heywood by his illustrious friend, and embodied in interludes, which made their appearance in type with the imprint of a typographer, who was connected by marriage with More, and whom it is not very fanciful to suppose that he had recommended to his brother humourist.

The two were, at one time, neighbours in Hertfordshire, if indeed Heywood was not actually domiciled with the Chancellor at one period of his life. They would be fond of collecting all the racy and diverting tales which fell in their way, to animate the conversation, as well as for literary use, and some of these were apt to be unsuited for dramatic purposes, while they might be thought deserving of preservation in some other form.

It does not strike me as at all improbable that the *Hundred Merry Tales*, looking at its great intrinsic merit, its relative freedom from grossness, the skilful manipulation of the narratives composing the series and their mainly original cast, and, lastly, the laconic and uncommercial title under which the book was ushered into publicity, that the collection was made by John Heywood with the assistance, possibly at the instigation, of Sir Thomas More, and committed to the press by More's kinsman in the same way that one or other of the two Rastells gradually executed the bulk of the publications of both authors. I propose to draw together the two or three scattered circumstances, which first led me to surmise that, in the most ancient and most interesting body of *facetiæ* in our own or any other language, the writer of *Utopia* and his jocund acquaintance—both alike the favourites of kings—were intimately concerned ; and it will be granted, I hope, that for this experimental attribution there is much more solid ground than ordinary conjecture.

Without any note of the year, but presumably in 1519, and at all events prior to the appearance of the *Tales*, John Rastell printed the Interlude of the *Four Elements*. This piece is usually regarded as anonymous ; and I cannot go so far as to positively lift the veil from the authorship. But it is curious enough that No. 19 of the *Tales* treats " Of the iiii. clemētys where they soulde sone be found." The affinity of title and subject may amount to nothing, although it is to be borne in mind that the dramatic profession, at this time, had very few followers, and that the topic was a peculiar one. But, independently of all that, there is a link between the little entry in the old story-book and the interlude of a far more pronounced character. In the play occurs the following passage :—

> " *Humanity.* Thou art a mad guest, by this light !
> *Sensual Appetite.* Yea, Sir, it is a fellow that never fails—
> But canst get my master a dish of quails ?
> Small birds, swallows, or wagtails ?
> They be light of digestion.
> *Tavener.* Light of digestion ? for what reason ?
> *Sen.* For physic putteth this reason thereto,

> Because those birds fly to and fro,
> And be continual moving.
> *Tav.* Then know I of a lighter meat than that.
> *Hu.* I pray thee, tell me what.
> *Ta.* If ye will needs know at short and long,
> It is even a woman's tongue,
> For that is ever stirring."

Now, No. 9 of the Tales speaks "of hym that sayd that a womans tong was lightest met of degestion." It purports to be a London story ; and the question arises, whether the compiler of the jest-book borrowed from the interlude, or the dramatist merely employed in the latter material which he had by him, and subsequently included in the *Tales.*[1] My own view is that the two passages are sufficiently like to have proceeded from the same source, and sufficiently different to make the hypothesis allowable, that the one was a dramatized development of the other, rather than that the jest was borrowed from the piece ; and I should, moreover, be inclined to put on the same footing the parallel between the interlude of the *Four Elements* and the ninth story in the book before us. There is altogether a cross-thread of testimony, which can be, at any rate, hardly otherwise than worth the space which it has cost to set it forth, and the more so, since we may have thus succeeded in removing the common mystery, which has hitherto hung over the production both of play and jest-book ; nor, in estimating the facts represented, ought we on any account to forget the condition of the press and the stage under Henry VIII., and how widely it differed from their aspect under Elizabethan and Stuart rule.

In the first moiety of the sixteenth century, the individuals in England capable of conceiving and carrying out such performances as the *Hundred Merry Tales* and the interludes of Heywood were countable on the fingers of one's hand ; and even in the absence of the remarkable coincidence which I have above indicated, the sponsorship for all works of the kind really lies within a very narrow range. It was not then as it was in and after the days of Shakespear, when a crowd of adventurers

---

[1] I refer the reader, for the original of the story, to the Notes.

swamped the market with their competitive labours. In 1526, the buyers and readers of miscellaneous literature were chiefly to be found among courtiers and scholars, and if Beatrice had actually had the *Tales* under her eyes, it is excessively unlikely that her mother ever beheld a copy.

Having regard to the unique brevity of the title to the collection, the abstinence from prefatory comment and the unbroken silence on the quarter whence the MS. was obtained, I should, if the names of Heywood and More were given to me, adjudge the book to More rather than to Heywood; because, in the case of Heywood, the anonymity could have no meaning, whereas a man in a high official capacity might not have chosen to identify himself with a miscellany containing so many censures on the Church. Two poetical trifles had, during his earlier years, stolen into print without his name, perhaps without his sanction : *The Merry Jest how a Serjeant would learn to be a friar*,[1] and *the Book of Lady Fortune ;*[2] and he had composed a series of stanzas illustrating the stages of human life for some hangings in his father's house.[3] *Jeux d'esprit* and light literature accorded with his taste, if not consonant with the dignity of his legal position.

I discern another corroboration of my theory in the sources to which the editor or adapter of the *Tales* went, where he drew from prior books, for they were just the class of literature to which the attention of scholars only would have been attracted. I beg to mention the *Summa Prædicantium* of Johannes de Bromyard and the *Joci ac Sales* of Luscinius, the latter bearing date 1524, two years before the appearance of the English collection, and a sort of volume which Desiderius Erasmus of Rotterdam might have sent across the sea to divert his Chelsea correspondent.

No. 19 of the *Tales* in the issue of 1526 seems to follow the cue of No. 8, and to be in the same misogynous vein ; and in the

---

[1] Hazlitt's *Popular Poetry*, iii. Warton does not speak favourably of this piece ; but I confess that it seems to me very entertaining and clever.

[2] Hazlitt's *Fugitive Tracts*, 1875, 1st Series.

[3] Warton's *H. of E. Poetry*, 1871, iv., 91.

former, as well as in No. 62, *Of the man that had the dome wyfe*, the aspen leaf is associated with the woman's tongue, though in a different sense.

If my idea as to the association of More with the *Tales* of 1526 be of any value, it may be an aid, in following the clue thus afforded, to remind the reader that, amid the multiplicity of topics embraced, there are several articles of a traditional cast, appertaining to the very commencement of the Tudor era, when More himself was a mere youth. I am looking at the anecdotes about the Welsh and Justice Vavasour, which belong to the fifteenth, rather than to the sixteenth, century; and these might have been communicated by his father Sir John More, or picked up in conversation with the old judge's friends. The advent to the throne of a prince of Cambro-British blood had led to a great scramble for places of profit among the Taffyhood and to the migration of considerable numbers to London, where their *gaucheries* laid them open to ridicule and their predatory tastes to chastisement.

At the same time, the suspected and proposed ascription of the volume cannot very well be pushed farther than a claim on behalf of More and his friend as contributors to its contents; for that there was a third hand in the affair—probably that of the printer and editor—certain expressions seem clearly to denote, and, for instance, in the anecdote about a man fully as celebrated as More himself, neither the latter nor Heywood could surely have described the antagonist of Wolsey as "*one* master Skelton, a poet laureat."

The *Hundred Merry Tales* were probably recommended to the compiler, as regards the complement, by the *Decameron* of Boccaccio, which had not yet been rendered into English, but was, of course, familiar to scholars in the original language. It has been often observed that in the old times a certain mystic affection existed for odd numbers, and that thence sprang the Three Fates, the Nine Muses, the Nine Sybilline Books, the Seven Wise Men, and so forth; but, as a matter of fact, the decimal and its multiples were nearly as usual, and even in the Scriptures we get the Ten Wise and Foolish Virgins, the Forty Years in the Wilderness, the Ten Commandments, the

Twelve Tables of the Mosaic Law, and the Twelve Judges of Israel. At all events, in early romantic lore no occult significance was attached to odd or even numbers ; but a century was not an unfrequent total.

One criterion of the special excellence of the *Hundred Tales,* 1526, is the manifest declension in merit of the *Merry Tales and Quick Answers,* which appeared a few years later in imitation of them, and which are equally entitled to be called Shakespear's Jest-Book, inasmuch as the trick of the boy on the blind man (No. 131) is quoted in the same drama, in which an incidental allusion occurs to the anterior publication.

The *Tales and Quick Answers,* by whomsoever they were brought together, are far more academical in their tone and complexion than the undertaking, in which I have attempted to trace the helping hand of More ; and this test is more applicable to the second edition (1567) than to the first of or about 1530. Yet, on the other hand, there is a certain proportion of matter in this volume germane in character and equal in interest to any found in the predecessor ; and one might be apt to indulge in a speculation, whether the editor or publisher had access to unused portions of the original MS., if it were not the case that the supplemental stories first added, so far as we at present know, in 1567 exhibit a similar admixture of the vernacular with the classical, of anecdotes of the ancients with humorous traits connected with the current or previous reign—little waifs of hearsay or report, which were calculated to lend a fillip to the book, at the same time that the citations from Plutarch and Lucian helped to communicate to the pages an odour of the ink-horn, acceptable to the more erudite ; but it is notable that no mention of Erasmus is made in the *Hundred Tales* nor in the first impression of the *Tales and Quick Answers,* although four consecutive items in the second known issue of the latter refer to him and his alleged heresies in a way which shews that the compiler was a friend to the Reformed Church, even if not that those insertions had formed part of some intermediate edition prior to the official establishment of Protestantism in England.

In the interlude of the *Four Elements* (1519), Tom Couper is introduced as a random name by one of the characters ; in the *Merry Tales*, No. 53, Master Cooper occurs in the same sort of way, unless the jest was the report of a matter of fact. This is a very insignificant rivet in the chain of supposed relationship between our two earliest jest-books and one of our most ancient dramatic productions of its class ; but I jot it down for what it may be worth as a minor factor ; and, once more, as regards the identity of sources from which the *Tales* of 1526 and a portion of those of the second collection or series were by possibility derived, there is the evident correlation between No. 20 of the former work and No. 54 of the latter, of which both came from some one conversant with Vavasour and his eccentricities. A still more powerful plea for the notion that the two volumes had a common editor is the striking similarity of treatment and style, and the uniformity of tone toward the church and the female sex.

The popularity of the *Tales* in our hands survived, more or less, down to the time of Elizabeth, and there are traces, both in the Stationers' Register and in the literature of the period, of editions of the work, of which not so much as an unique copy has descended to us. The *Hundred Merry Tales*, properly so named, and the *Merry Tales and Quick Answers* seem after a while to have been occasionally confounded from the tolerably close correspondence in the titles ; thus Sir John Harington, in his *Apology (for the Metamorphosis of Ajax)*, 1596, observes:

"Ralph Horsey, Knight, the best housekeeper in Dorsetshire, a good free-holder, a deputie Lieutenant. Oh, sir, you keep hauks and houndes, and hunting horses : it may be som madde fellowe will say, you must stand up to the chinne, for spending five hundred poundes, to catch hares, and Partridges, that might be taken for five poundes." Then comes this note in the margin : " according to the tale in the hundred Mery Tales."

But Harington's memory deceived him, for he meant to refer to No. 52 of the *Merry Tales and Quick Answers*, where we meet with a story " Of hym that healed franticke men ; " and it is accompanied by this moral : " This tale toucheth such young gentyll menne, that dispende ouer moche good on haukes, and other trifils."

The allusion to the Henry VIII. book in works of later date, and even the entries at Stationers' Hall, do not absolutely prove that the volume was ever republished after 1526. But Laneham, in his *Letter from Kenilworth,* 1575, enumerates the *Tales* among the contents of the library of Captain Cox of Coventry, which, as the writer usually cites books and tracts of contemporary date, may possibly serve as a piece of collateral evidence in favour of the existence at one period of impressions now unknown.

Taylor the Water-Poet, too, cites the *Tales* as one of the works of reference employed by him in the composition of *Sir Gregory Nonsense his Newes from no Place,* 1622, as if even at that epoch they had not quite lost their reputation.

As the plan adopted is to place the HUNDRED MERRY TALES before the public for the first time, in the very form and semblance which it wore at its issue from the press of John Rastell 360 years since, the original text is given without the slighest alteration in any respect, and the Additional Tales, in the other edition by Rastell without date, are inserted in the Appendix.

The Notes, for a few of which I am indebted to the erudition of Dr. Oesterley, are mainly illustrative of the sources whence the Anecdotes were taken, where they are not, as frequently happens, original, and occasionally of the later application of them in the books of the people, which cheered the life of the seventeenth and eighteenth centuries. But I did not consider it worth while to trace the stories through all their modern developments and modifications.

The reprint of *A C. Mery Talys* from the dateless edition of Rastell under the care of Mr. S. W. Singer, and from that text again in *Old English Jest Books,* 1864, is not literally accurate, as I discovered to my regret, when the original copy was lent to me many years ago by Mr. Halliwell-Phillipps.

W. C. H.

*Barnes Common, Surrey.*
*March,* 1887.

# APPENDIX.

THE three stories from the undated edition not included in that of 1526.[1]

### ¶ *Of the courtear that ete the hot custarde.* xcvii.

¶ A CERTAYNE merchaunt and a courtear, *being upon a time together* at dyner hauing a hote custerd, *the courtear being* somwhat homely of maner toke *parte of it and put it* in hys mouth, whych was so hote that made him *shed teares. The* merchaunt, lokyng on him, thought that he had *ben weeping, and asked hym why* he wept. This curtear, not wyllynge [it] to be known *that he had brent his* mouth with the hote custerd, answered and said : sir, q*uod he I had* a brother whych dyd a certayn offence wherfore he was hanged ; *and, chauncing* to think now vppon his deth, it maketh me to wepe. This merchaunt thought the courtear had said trew, and anon after the merchaunt was disposid to ete *of the custerd,* and put a sponefull of it in his mouth, and brent his mouth also, that his *eyes watered.* This courtear, that perceuyng, spake to the merchaunt and seyd : sir, quod *he, pray* why do ye wepe now ? The merchaunt perseyued how he had *bene deceiued* and said : mary, quod he, I wepe, because thou wast not hangid, *when that* thy brother was hangyd.

### ¶ *Of the thre pointes belonging to a shrewd wyfe.* xcix.

¶ A YONG man, that was desirous to haue a wyf, cam to a company *of Phi*losofers which were gadred to gider, requiring them to gif *him their opinion* howe he might chose him sich a wyf that wer no shrew. These *Philos*ofers with gret study and delyberacion determinid and shewd this man that there *were iii espe*cial pointes, wherebi he shuld

---

(1) The matter in italics is supplied from conjecture.

sure know if a woman were a shrew. The *i point is* that if a woman have a shril voyce, it is a gret token that she is a shrew. The ii point is that, if a woman have a sharp nose, then most commenly she is a shrew. *The* iii point that neuer doth mis is[1] that if she were [a] kerchefer,[2] ye may be sure she is a shrew.

¶ *Of the man that paynted the lamb upon his wyfes bely.* c.

❦ A CONNING painter ther was dwelling in London, which had a fayre yong wife, and for thingis that he had to do went ouer se ; but because he was somwhat jelous, he praed his wyfe to be content, that he might paint a lamb upon her bely, and praed her it might remain ther, til he cam home again ; wherewith she was content. After which lamb so painted he departid ; and sone after that, a lusti yong merchaunt, a bacheler, came and woed his wyf, and obteined her fauor, so that she was content he shuld lye with her ; which resortid to her and had his plesure oftymes ; and on time he toke a pensell, and to the lamb he painted ii hornys, wening to the wif that he had but refreshed the old painting. Than at the last, about a yere after, her husband cam home again, and the first night he lay with his wyfe, he loked uppon his wifes bely, and saw the ii hornes painted there. He said to his wif, that some other body had been besy there, and made a new painting : for the picture that he painted had no hornes and and this hath hornes ; to whome this wif shortly

\* \* \* \* \* \* \*

*cetera desunt.*

(1) *The iii point is that never mis that, &c.*, old copy, according to Singer.

(2) The kerchief, which was a very costly item of ladies' dress during the Tudor and Stuart times, formed part of the head-gear, and was doubtless worn in a different way by different persons. In the *New Courtly Sonet of sthe Lady Greensleeves*, printed in Robinson's "Handful of Pleasant Delites," 1584, the lover says to his mistress :—

> " I bought three kerchers to thy head,
> That were wrought fine and gallantly:
> I kept thee both at board and bed,
> Which cost my purse well-favourdly."

# NOTES.

TALE I., f. i. *ro.* *Comande me.*] The jest turns here on the double meaning of the words *command* and *doubt* or *dout.* In French and early English the former signifies either *to command* or *to commend.*

TALE II., f. i. *ro.*] This does not occur in the undated edition.

TALE III., f. i. *ro.*] This is a very common story. It may be found, told somewhat differently, in Boccaccio, 7th Day, 7th Novel, in the *Pecorone* of Ser Giovanni Fiorentino, in Barbazan's *Fabliaux,* where it is related of the Bourgeoise d'Orleans, and in the *Facetiae* of Poggius (*de Muliere quæ virum defraudavit*). The imitations in more modern works are innumerable.

TALE IV., f. i. *vo.*] In the undated edition this is described as the tale ¶ Of John Adroyns in the dyuils apparell. A story very similar, as an actual incident, is inserted in the *Autobiography* of Wallett the Queen's Jester, 1870. See John Heywood's *Epigrams, &c.,* Spenser Soc. ed., p. 214.

At the bottom of fol. i. *verso* there is in the original copy an imperfection in the text after *broke,* where the words *his nek,* found in the other edition, are required to complete the sense.

TALE V., f. ii. *vo.*] In the undated edition this is ¶ *Of the ryche man and his two sonnes.* It is mutilated.

TALE VI., f. ii. *vo.*] Compare Les Cent Nouvelles Nouvelles, No. 62 ; Celio Malespini, *Novelle,* 1609, nov. 2 ; Decker and Webster's *Northward Hoe,* 1607 (Webster's works, by Hazlitt, 1857, i, 178—9).

TALE VII., f. iii. *ro.*] Not in the undated edition. This is a well known story in German ; and compare Taylor's *Wit and Mirth,* 1630, p. 101, and Dr. Oesterley's edit., 1866, p. 14.

TALE IX., f. iii. *vo.*] This tale has served me as a clue to the probable or supposed authorship of the book. See what I have said in the *Introduction.* Dr. Oesterley observes:—The source of this tale is Johannes de Bromyard, Summa Prædicantium, s. l. & a. fol. Litt. L. v. § 21, Exempl. i.: " Patet per hiſtoriam qua fertur infirmum reſpondiſſe medico dicenti: quod comederet de parte piſcium caude propinquiori: quia ſanior erat pars: quia plus mouebatur : ergo inquit infirmus: lingua uxoris mee ſaniſſima eſt, quia continue mouetur," See also Wright, " Latin Stories from MSS. of the 13th and 14th Centuries," 1842, No. 132: " DeLinguis Mulierum."

Another verſion is found in Vincent of Beauvais, *Speculum Morale,* Duaci, 1624. fol. 86: Narratvr de quodam, quod cum ipſe in mari haberet vxorem ſuam ſecum lingualam, grauem ad tolerandum : cum imminente tempeſtate clamatum eſſet a nautis, quod grauiora de naui proiicerentur, ille exhibuit vxorem dicens quod in tota naui non erat aliquid grauius lingua eius. It is imitated in H. Bebelii Facetiæ, opuſcula, s. l. & a. (circa 1512\, 4°. fign. Ce verſo: De quodam in tempeſtate maris deprehenſo (de alio)," and repeated in Joh. Gaſtius " Convivalium Sermonum, tom. i. p. 281, Baſil. 1549.

TALE XI., f. iiii. *ro.*] Compare Bebelius, *Facetiæ,* sign. Gg2, "De muliere citiſsime nubente poſt obitum primi viri." It is versified in the *Uncasing of Machivils Instructions to his sonne,* 1613, sign. C3 :

> " If thou be slow to speake, as one I knew,
> Thou wouldst assure thy selfe my counsels true ;
> Hee ,too late) finding her upon her knees
> In Church, where yet her husbands coorse she sees,
> Hearing the Sermon at his funerall,
> Longing to behold his buriall,
> This sutor being toucht with inward love,
> Approached neare his lovely sute to move,
> Then stooping downe he whispered in her eare
> Saying he bore her love, as might appeare,
> In that so soone he shewed his love unto her,
> Before any else did app[r'och to woo her,
> Alass ,said she) your labour is in vaine,
> Last night a husband I did entertaine."

See *Notes and Queries,* 3rd Series, v. 491. Stories of this kind are of very common occurrence in the modern collections of facetiæ.

TALE XII., f. iiii. *ro.*] See *Retrospective Review,* New Series, ii, 326, where it is said that the tale of the miller with the golden thumb was still a favourite in Yorkshire in 1854. There is a Somersetshire proverb, "An honest miller hath a golden thumb, but none but a cuckold can see it." The reader may refer to my *Popular Antiquities of Great Britain,* 1870, iii, 342, where a good deal of information on this subject is collected.

> " When Davie Diker diggs, and dallies not,
> When Smithes shoo horses, as they would be shod,
> When millers toll not with a golden thumb."—
> Gascoigne's *Steel Glas,* 1576.
> (Works by Hazlitt, ii, 211 and Note)

TALE XIII., f. iiii. *ro.*] Dr. Oesterley enumerates two German imitations of this Story in his edition, 1866, p. 22-3. But compare Ellis's *Original Letters,* 2nd Series, ii, 99, 101, for a glimpse of the disturbed condition of Ireland at this very juncture.

TALE XIV., f. iiii. *vo.*] The Archdeacon here intended was probably Richard Rawson, who held the Archdeaconry of Essex from 1303 to 1343 (Le Neve's *Fasti,* ed. Hardy, ii, 336 .

TALE XVI., f v. *10.*] Compare Poggii *Facetiæ,* ap. *Opera,* 1538, fol. 439.—De quodam paſtore ſimulatim confitente. Paſtor ouium ex ea regni Neapolitani ora, quæ olim iatrociniis operam dabant ſemel confeſſorem adijt, ſua peccata dicturus. Cum ad facerdotis genua procubuiſſet, parce mihi 'inquit ille lachrimans , pater mi, quoniam grauiter deliqui. Cum juberet dicere quid eſſet. Atque ille ſepius id verbum interaſſet, tanquam qui nepharium admiſiſſet ſcelus. Tamden hortatu facerdotis, ait ſe, cum caſeum faceret, iciunj tempore, expreſſuri lactis guttas quaſdam quas non fpreuiffet in os defilijffe. Tum facerdos qui mores illius patriæ noffet fubridens, cum dixiffet illum dcliquiffe qui quadragefimam non feruaffet, quæfivit numquid aliis obnoxius effet pcccatis? Abnuente, paflor rogauit num cum alijs pafloribus quenquam peregrinum ut mos effet illius regionis tranfeuntem fpoliaffet aut peremiffet? Sæpius, inquit, utraque in re cum reliquis fum verfatus. Sed iflud, ait, apud nos ita efl confuetum, ut nulla confcientia fiat. . . . ."

TALE XVIII., f. v. *vo.*] The fource of this tale is perhaps the fabliau Etula, in Legrand d'Auffy, " Fabliaux," tom. iii. p. 77 ; better in Sinner, "Catalogus Codicum MSS." tom. iii.p. 379, No. 14. It is also related in the Scala Celi,1480, de furto quinto, fol. 101 verfo: " Legitur quod cum duo latrones conveniffent ut furarentur, unus nuces et alter carnes ; perveniens ad fores ecclefiæ qui furatus fuerat nuces, incepit frangere et comedere eas ibi. Cujus fonitum audiens ille, qui cuflodiebat ecclefiam, credens quod dæmon ingreffus efl clauflrum et cuidam claudo, qui ire non potuit et forti ruflico videnti nunciavit. Et dum ingreffi fuiffent ecclefiam, latro comedebat nuces, credens quod effet focius fuus, qui portaret arietem, incepit clamare : Eftne bene pinguis quem portas? Tunc ruflicus territus qui portabat claudum, credens quod effet dæmon : Nefcio fi efl pinguis vel macer, fed nunc relinquo eum vobis. Et projecto claudo ad terram tibiam aliam fibi fregit." Alfo in Joh. de Bromyard, " Summa prædicantium," Litt. O, ii, § 6.

Imitations are : J. Pauli, "Schimpff und Ernfl," Straffburg, 1535, fol. No. 76, fol. 15 ; G. Wickram, " Der Rollwagen," s. l. 1557, No. 67, ( Frankf. 1590, fol. 72 : " Wie zween Dieb einem Pfaffen das Podagram vertriben"), reprinted in Wackernagel, " Deutfches Lefebuch," Wickram ; Hans Sachs, " Gedichte," vol. ii. l. 4, fol. 73, Nürnberg, 1592, fol.: " Die zwen diebifchen Bachanten in dem Toden Kercker." —*Oesterley.*

TALE XIX., f. vi. *vo.*] Dr. Oesterley notes some modern German imitations of this anecdote. But it may perhaps be read advantageously with the Interlude of 1519 in my Dodsley, vol. i.

TALE XX., f. vii. *ro.*] The judge Vavasour here mentioned was probably John Vavasour, a member of an old Yorkshire family, who was Recorder of York, 1st Henry VII., and became a justice of the Common Pleas in 1490. See Foss, v. 78-9.

Compare *Merry Tales and Quicke Answers*, No. 54.

TALE XXII., f. vii. *vo.*] Dr. Oesterley says that this story originates in the *Summa Prædicantium* of Johannes de Bromyard, and is found in Holkot. *Super Libros Sapientiæ*, 1489, fol. iii. He also cites imitations of it in modern German works of later date.

TALE XXIV., f. viii. *ro.*] This is repeated in the *Merrie Tales of the Wise men of Gotam* in my "Shakespeare Jest-Books," 1864, iii. No edition of the latter so early as 1526 is known or likely; and it is within the limits of probability that the insertion of this anecdote suggested the formation of a series of analogous noodledoms. 1526 was also before Borde's time. Here we have only three simpletons ; but the number was subsequently extended to twelve.

TALE XXVI., f. viii. *ro.*] This story is slightly mutilated in the undated copy.

TALE XXVII., f. ix. *ro* ] Dr. Oesterley aptly remarks : " To take a nap at fermon or at church is quite a common faying in Germany, so common indeed, that a technical term, ' Kirchenfchlaf,' has been given to this particular nap."

The anecdote is quoted by Latimer in his fixth fermon before Edward VI., 1549; it is imitated in the *Conceits of Hobson*, 1607.

As regards St. Thomas of Acres, a contemporary writer, Skelton, in his *Colin Clout* (Works, by Dyce, i, 357), says:—

> "At the Austen fryers
> They count us for lyers:
> And at Saynt Thomas of Akers
> They carpe us lyke crakers."

TALE XXVIII., f. ix. *ro.*] This item is a mere indecipherable fragment in the other edition.

TALE XXXI., f. ix. *vo.*] Borde, in his *Book of the Introduction of Knowledge* (1542), makes his Welshman say of himself:—

> " I am a Welshman, and do dwel in Wales;
> I have loued to serche budgets, and loke in males."

The Welsh have ceased to be borderers, but their celebrity for cheating, lying, and drinking, as well as a certain stolid malignity, has not deserted them. Had they been papists, instead of being mainly Protestant Dissenters, they would have been found even more troublesome than the Irish, to whom they are in many respects inferior.

TALES XXXIII.—IV., f. x *ro.*] Both these are imperfect in the undated copy, where they are Nos. 31—2.

TALE XXXV., f. x. *vo.*] "Dr. *South*, visiting a gentleman one morning, was ask'd to stay Dinner, which he accepted of ; the Gentleman stept into the next Room and told his Wife, and desired she'd provide something extraordinary. Hereupon she began to murmur and scold, and make a thousand Words ; till at length her husband, provok'd at her Behaviour, protested, that if it was not for the stranger in the next Room, he would kick her out of Doors. Upon which the Doctor, who heard all that passed, immediately stept out, crying, *I beg, Sir, you'll make no Stranger of me.*"—*Complete London Jester*, ed. 1771, p. 73.

TALE XXXVI., f. x. *vo.*] Too fragmentary in the other copy to make out the text or sense. Dr. Oesterly points out an analogue in Des Periers, *Nouvelles Recreations*, 1735, i, Nouv. 23, " Du jeune fils qui fit valoir le beau Latin que son Curé lui avoit monstré."

TALE XXXVIII., f. x. *vo.*] In *El Conde Lucanor*, an early collection of Spanish stories by Juan Manuel, a similar division of a woman occurs, except that there the servant girl has only two claimants, the Virtue and the Vice, of whom the latter selects the lower half. The same idea has been used in German literature.

TALE XL., f. xi. *vo.*] This story is in the *Fabliaux* under the title of *Les Trois Aveugles de Compiegne*, in Straparola, &c., and two variants occur in Scoggin's Jests. *Old English Jest Books*, 1864, ii, where I mention that the same material is worked up again in *Hobson's Conceits*, 1607.

Sarcinet, at the period to which the original anecdote points, was a texture, which only certain persons were entitled to wear. See note by Sir Harris Nicolas to the *Privy Purse Expenses of Elizabeth of York*, p. 220.

TALE XLI., f. xi. *vo.*] This is repeated in the *Merrie Tales of Skelton*, No. 6 ; but there capons are substituted for the pheasants. A similar anecdote occurs in the *Jests of Scoggin*. See *Old English Jest Books*, 1864, ii, pp. 10, 130.

TALE XLII., f. xii. *vo.*] A carter, when this book was published, and long after indeed, was not necessarily what we should now understand from the term, as ordinary vehicles for the conveyance of passengers—in fact, carriages—were down to the Jacobean period of a form very similar to our carts. See *Sussex Archæological Collections*, i, 178, and my note in the *Antiquary*, XIV, 252.

TALE XLIII., f. xii. *vo.*] This is No. 33 of the other copy.

TALE XLIV., f. xiii., *ro.*] In the other copy this is No. 42. It does not occur in the Table to the original edition, though Singer, and after him the present writer, inserted the heading both there and before the tale, which is found in the *Summa Prædicantium* of Johannes de Bromyard, as follows:—"De quodam domino, qui fatuum fuum infirmum frequenter cum per illum tranfiret, confortari folebat. dicendo: Spera in deo: ibis ad cœlum. Cui ille femper refpondit : nolo illuc ire : a quo cum uno die quereret, quare nollet illuc ire, refpondit : quia volo ire ad infernum ; quare ? inquit; quia, inquit, diligo te : & ficut fui tecum in vita, ita volo tecum effe in morte. & poft mortem: & quia tu ibis ad infernum : ita volo ego ratione focietatis. Cui dominus : quomodo fcis quod ego illud vadam ? quia, inquit. tota patria loquitur fic. dicentes. quod tu es peffimus homo. et ideo ibis ad infernum: Et in veritate: qui malus homo fuit prius. ex verbis illius compunctus: optime fe poftea correxit."

TALE XLVIII., f. xiii. *vo.*] This anecdote is also in the *Summa Prædicantium*, a book very likely, by the by, to have fallen in Sir Thomas More's way; but probably the original germ is the Latin *Fabliau* printed by Wright in his selection of Latin Stories, 1842, No. 129, under the title of "De rustico et simia." The text is incomplete in the copy of the other impression. The imitations of it are very numerous.

TALE XLIX., f. xiiii. *ro.*] This is also mutilated in the copy of Rastell's other edition. Dr. Oesterley has collected a large body of imitations and analogues (*Shakesp. Jest Book*, 1866, p. 83—4).

TALE LI., f. xiiii. *vo.*] Imperfect in the undated copy.

TALE LII., f. xv. *ro.*] The Church of St. Nicholas Shambles was in Newgate Market ; it was demolished at the Reformation.

TALE LIV., f. xv. *ro.*]

> Thus these sysmatickes,
> And lowsy lunatickes,
> With spurres and prickes
> Call true men heretickes.
> They finger their fidles,
> And cry in quinibles,
> Away these bibles,
> For they be but ridles !
> And give them Robyn Whode,
> For to red howe he stode,
> In mery grene wode,
> Where he gathered good,
> Before Noyes Floodd.
>
> *The Image of Ipocrysy*, part 3.

TALE LV., f. xv. *vo.*] Defective in the undated copy. The story is adopted by the compiler of *Scoggins Jests*, where we are told, "How the Priest said: *Deus qui viginti filii tui*, when he should have said *Deus qui unigeniti*," but the text differs.

TALE LVI., f. xvi. *ro.*] The miracle play in Warwickshire was one of the series performed at Coventry, but does not occur in the printed collection entitled Ludus

Coventriæ. There is, however, the "Emission of the Holy Ghost," inserted among the Chester Mysteries, edited by Wright for the Shakespeare Society, ii, 134 :—

### "*Petrus.*

I beleeve in God omnipotente,
That made heaven and eirth and firmament,
With fteadfaft harte and trewe intente,
And he is my comforte.

### *Andreas*

And I beleeve more I be lente,
In Jefu his fonne from heaven fente,
Vereye Chrift that us hath kente,
And is our elders lore.

### *Jacobus Major.*

And I beleeve, with bofte,
In Jefu Chrifte. in mighteft mofte,
Confeveith through the holye ghofte,
And borne was of Marye.

### *Johannes.*

And I beleeve. as I cane fee,
That under Pilate fuffred he,
Skourged and nayled on roode tree,
And buryed was his fayre bodye.

### *Thomas.*

And I beleeve. and fouth can tell,
That he ghoftly wente to helle :
Delivered his that there did dwell,
And rofe the thirde daie.

### *Jacobus Minor.*

And I beleeve fully this,
That he fteyed up to heaven bleffe,
And on his fathers righte hand is,
To raigne for ever and aye.

### *Philipus.*

And I beleeve, with harte fteadfafte,
That he will come at the lafte,
And deeme mankinde as he has cafte,
Bouth the quicke and the dead.

### *Barthelemewe.*

And I beleffe fhalbe mofte
In vertue of the holye ghoft,
And through his helpe, without bofte,
My life I thinke to leade.

*Mathieus.*

And I beleeve, through Godes grace,
Suche beleffe as holye chourch has,
That Godes bodye graunted us was
To ufe in forme of bredde.

*Symon.*

And I beleve with devocion
Of fynne to have remiffion,
Through Chriftes bloode and paffion,
And heaven, when I am dead.

*Jude.*

And I beleeve, as all we mon,
In the generall refurrexcion
Of eiche bodye, when Chrifte is borne
To deme bouth good and evill.

*Matheus.*

And I beleeve, as all we maye,
Everlaflinge life after my daye
In heaven to have ever and aye,
And fo overcome the devill."

TALE LVII., f. xvi. *vo.*] Dr. Oesterley here writes :—"The divifion of the Decalogue followed in this tale is taken from Exodus xx; it was adopted by the Council of Trent, and ufed by the whole Latin Church. Luther approved of it, and it is ftill in ufe with the entire Lutheran denomination. The divifion nowemployed by the Church of England is the fame which has always been ufed by the Greek Church. It was ftrongly recommended by Calvin in 1536, adopted by Bucer and the Tetrapolitans, and is to be found in any Englifh formulary fince 1537. Mr. Hazlitt's conjecture for the lacuna in his edition, p. 28, is therefore inadmiffible ; and this is more clearly fhown by the fact, that in his interpolation either the feventh or eight commandment is omitted. To judge from the undamaged paffages, however, there muft have been fome difference between Mr. Hazlitt's original and mine : the text of the mutilated copy cannot have read but thus : *The eighth, not to bear falfe witnefs againft thy neighbour.* THE NINTH AND TENTH, *not to couete nor defyre no mannes goodes vnlefully. Thou fhalt not defyre thy neyghbours wyfe,* &c., this being exactly the form, which was nearly exclufively ufed fince its acceptation by the Council of Trent Catechifm. It is likewife found in Mafkell's and Bifhop Hilfey's Primers.

The feven deadly fins have always been the fame, but their divifion is fometimes different. See Mr. Hazlitt's edition, p. 83, note ·2, and Mafkell's " Prymer," in " Monum. Ritual. Anglic." vol. ii. p. 178, London, 1846."

Richard Whitford, in his *Werke for Houfeholders,* firft printed before 1530, fays of the *Seven deadly Sins* :—"yet muft you have a leffon to teche your folkes to beware of the VII pryncipall fynnes, whiche ben communely called the feven dedely fynnes, but in dede they done call them wronge : for they be not alway dedely fynnes. Therefore they fholde be called capytall or pryncipall fynnes, and not dedely fynnes. These ben theyre names by ordere after our dyvyfion: Pryde, Envy, Wrath, Covetyfe, Glotony, Slouth, and Lechery."

TALE LVIII., f. xvi. *vo.*] A me'rical imitation of this is to be found in John Cotgrave's Wits Interpreter, ed. 1662, p. 286.

TALE LXII., f. xvii. *vo.*] This is introduced by Rabelais into his narrative, lib. 3, c. 34 ; but he puts a physician in the devil's place. A metrical version is found in the *Scholehouse of Women*, first printed about 1540. In the undated copy the text is imperfect.

TALE LXIII., f. xviii. *ro.*] It is by no means unlikely, as Dr. Oesterly first suggested, that the editor of *A C. Mery Talys* borrowed this from Ottomarus Luscinius, "Joci ac Sales miré festivi," 1524, No. 50, where however, it is related of Aristotle. There are later imitations.

TALE LXVI., f. xviii. *vo.*] In the Table to the undated copy, this purports to be told "of him that woulde gette the maystrye of his wyfe." The text is incomplete at the end ; but in the *Schoolhouse of Women* we have a metrical paraphrase, which supplies the deficiency:—

> " A husband man, having good trust
> His wife to him bad be agreeable,
> Thought to attempt if she had be reformable,
> Bad her take the pot, that sod over the fire,
> And set it aboove upon the astire.
> 　　She answered him : ' I hold thee mad,
> And I more fool, by Saint Martine;
> Thy dinner is redy, as thou me bad,
> And time it were that thou shouldst dine,
> And thou wilt not, I will go to mine.'
> ' I bid thee (said he) vere up the pot.'
> ' A ha ! (said she) I trow thou dote.'
> 　　Up she goeth for fear, at last,
> No question mooved where it should stand
> Upon his hed the pottage she cast,
> And heeld the pot still in her hand,
> Said and swore, he might her trust,
> She would with the pottage do what her lust."

TALE LXIX., f. xix. *vo.*] This is a very common and favourite hoax. In *Joake upon Joake*, 1721, it is inserted of Charles II., Nell Gwynn, and the Duchess of Portsmouth, the last being made the sufferer.

But the editor of the *Tales* was probably indebted to the *Joci ac Sales* of Luscinius, 1524, already cited, although their texts do not perfectly accord in the details. The incident occurs with a slight variation among the *Jests of Scogin.*

TALE LXX., f. xix. *vo.*] There is a similar story in *Tarlton's Newes out of Purgatory*. Both have the air of having had a common Italian origin.

TALE LXXI., f. xx. *ro.*] Dr. Oesterley (*Shakesp. Jest Book*, 1866, p. 122 ) adduces several comparatively late parallels, and adds—"A very fimilar ftory can be heard to this day in Germany: A waiter in theWeidenbufch Hotel in Frankfort o. M. propofes the following riddle to a Pruffian Lieutenant: It is not my brother, it is not my fifter, and yet it is my mother's child. The lieutenant gueffes and gueffes, until at laft the waiter tells him that it is himfelf. On the following day the lieutenant puts the fame riddle at an evening party. The whole company declares : That is your-felf, Lieutenant. No, Ladies and Gentlemen, it is the waiter at the Weidenbufch Hotel."

TALE LXXIII., f. xx. *vo.*] The village of Shottery, mentioned as the scene of this Jest, is about a mile from Stratford, between that town and Bordon Hill.

TALE LXXIV., f. xx. *vo.*] Undecipherable in the undated copy.

TALE LXXV., f. xx. *vo.*] The saying, which constitutes the *stamina* of this anecdote, is a different form of the one, that a thousand angels can stand on the point of a needle. Ward of Stratford, in his Diary, ed. 1839, p. 94., has this passage :— One querying another, whether a thousand angels might stand on the point of a needle, another replied, " That was a *needles* point."

TALE LXXVI., f. xx. *vo.*] Imperfect in the undated copy.

TALE LXXVIII., f. xxi. *vo.*] Borde, in the *Fyrst boke of the Introduction of Knowledge* (1542) puts into the mouth of the Welshman:—

" I do loue cause boby, good tosted chese."

TALE LXXX., f. xxi. *vo.*] In his *Discovery of Witchcraft*, 1584, ed. 1651, p. 191, Scot has copied this anecdote as follows :— " So it was, that a certain Sir John, with some of his company, once went abroad jetting, and in a moon-light evening, robbed a miller's weire and stole all his eeles. The poor miller made his mone to Sir John himself, who willed him to be quiet ; for he would so curse the theef, and all his confederates, with bell, book, and candel, that they should have small joy of their fish. And therefore the next Sunday, Sir John got him to the pulpit, with his surplisse on his back, and his stole about his neck, and pronounced these words following :—

> 'All you that have stolne the millers eeles,
> *Laudate Dominum de coelis,*
> And all they that have consented thereto,
> *Benedicamus Domino.'*

Lo (saith he), there is savce for your celes, my masters."

The text is too imperfect in the undated copy to ascertain the sense, and until the Göttingen one was discovered, the substantial transcript in Scot, which I first pointed out in my notes to *Old English Jest Books*, 1864, formed our only resource for a knowledge of the drift of the tale.

TALE LXXXI., f. xxi. *vo.*] Imperfect in the undated copy.

TALE LXXXII., f. xxii. *ro.*] Dr. Oesterley (*Shakespeare Jest Book*, 1866, p. 134) quotes an anecdote in the " Nouveaux Contes à rire," 1702, where a family of thieves steal a hog, kill it, and upon search being made for it, cover it with a cloth, and weep for it as for their father.

TALE LXXXIII., f. xxii. *ro.*] Very imperfect in the undated copy.

The same story occurs in the *Facetiæ* of Bebelius, according to Oesterley, under the title of " De insatia cuiusdam sacerdotis fabula perfaceta," and it is also found in the *Jests of Scogin*, from which I tried to supply the *lacunæ* in the text, before the Göttingen copy became known.

TALE LXXXIV., f. xxii. *ro.*] This and the three next are imperfect in the undated copy. No. 84 also occurs with variations in the *Jests of Scoggin*.

TALE LXXXIX., f. xxiii. *ro.*] This was the famous Sir Richard Whittington, who is commemorated in plays, poems, and ballads. Thomas Heywood thus introduces him into his drama entitled: *If you know not me, you know nobody*, 1606; it is a dialogue held between Hobson, the haberdasher of the Poultry, and Dr. Nowell, Dean of St. Paul's :—

> "*Dr. Now.* This Sir Richard Whittington, three times Mayor,
> Son to a knight, and 'prentice to a mercer,
> Began the library of Gray-friars in London,
> And his executors after him did build
> Whittington College, thirteen almshouses for poor men,
> Repair'd Saint Bartholomew's in Smithfield,
> Glazed the Guildhall, and built Newgate.
> *Hob.* Bones a me, then, I have heard lies ;
> For I have heard he was a scullion,
> And rais'd himself by venture of a cat.
> *Dr. Now.* They did the more wrong to the gentleman."

This, as well as the following story is defective in the other copy.

TALE XCI., f. xxiii. *vo.*] This story is omitted in the undated impression ; and it is one of the longest and best in the series.

TALE XCIV., f. xxiiii. *vo.*] The text of the undated copy is mutilated both in this and the next article.

TALE XCVII., f. xxv. *ro.*] This is also imperfect in the other copy.

TALE XCVIII., f. xxv. *ro.*] This story is peculiar to the edition of 1526, and the next "Of the northern man that was all hart," has all but perished in the other copy, merely a few illegible fragments remaining.

TALE C., f. xxvi. *ro.*] This is also incomplete in the undated copy.

APPENDIX.] Tales numbered 97, 99, and 100 in the undated copy are wanting in that of 1526. They are all more or less incomplete, the last terminating abruptly from the failure of the fragments of pasteboard to supply the end.

# INDEX.

28 *Index.*

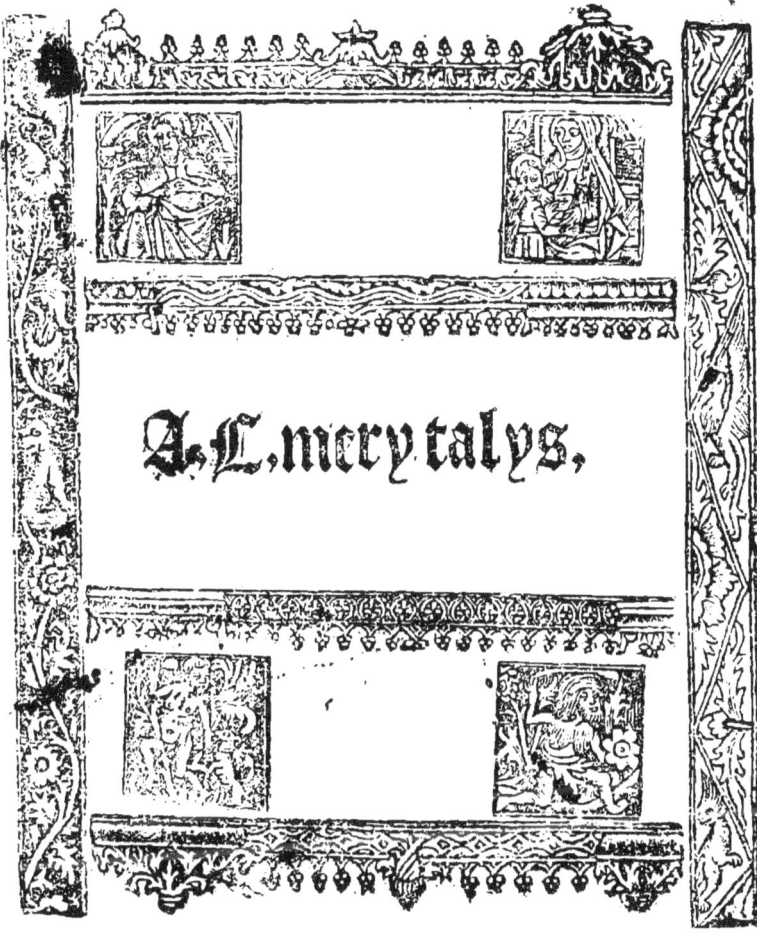

# A.C. mery talys,

A.ii.

**finis.**

Certayn Curat in the contrey there was that preched
in the pulpit of the ten commandementys Seyng that
there were ten cōmaūdemētes that euery man ought
to kepe / ₮ he that brake any of tl̄ē / cōmytted greuous
syn/how be it he sayd that somtyme it was dedly syn ₮
somtyme benyall/ But when it was dedly syn ₮ when
benyall/ there were many doutis therin And a mylnet
ā yong mā a mad felow that cam seldom to churcl̄ / ₮ had ben at very sewe
sermōs or none in all his lyfe answerd hym thā shortly this wyse. I meruel
master parson that ye say ther be so many cōmaūdemēts ₮ so many doutys
for I neuer hard tell but of u.cōmandemēts that is to say cōmaūte me to
you ₮ cōmaūde me fro you. Nor I neuer herd tell of no doutis but twayn
that ys to say dout the candell. ₮ dout the fyre. At which answere all the peo
ple fell a laughynge.

℟ By this tale a man may well preyue that they that be brought vp wtout
out leryng or good maner shall neuer be, but rude and bestely all though
they haue good naturall wyttys.

A a tyme there was a Joly Citesyn walkyng in the cōtrey for
sport which met with a solysh prest/₮ in dirysyō in cōmunycacō
cald hym syr John. this prest vnderstonding his mockyng calde
him master rafe/why quod the cytesyn doste thou call me master rafe/mary
quod the prest why callyst me syr John. Then quod the cytesen I call the syr
John becawse euery solysh preste most comonly is calde sir John/Mary qd
the prest ₮ I call the master rafe becau̅se euery proud Cocold most comenly
is callyd master Rafe. At the which answer all that were by laught a pace
becau̅se dyuers there supposyd the same cytesen to be a cokcold in dede.

℟ By thys tale ye may se that he that delyteh to deryde ₮ laughe other
to skorne is somtyme hym selfe more derydyd.

wyfe ther was which had apointed her prētys to com to her bed
in the night which seruāt had long word her to haue his plesure
which acordige to the apoitmēt cā to her bed syde i the night her
hu̅sbād lyeng by her ₮ when she preuyd hym ther she caught hi by the hād ₮
hyld hym sast ₮ incōtinēt wakened her hu̅sbōd ₮ sayd / Sir it is so ye haue
a fals ₮ an vntru seruāt to you which is william your prentys ₮ hath lōge
woord me to haue his plesur/₮ becawse I coud nat auoyde his importunate
eequest I haue appoityd hym this night to met me in the gardē i the herber
₮ yf ye wyll aray your self in myn aray ₮ go theder ye shall se the pūf therof
₮ then ye may rebuke hym as ye thike best by your dysfrecyon / this husbād
thus aduertised by his wyfe/ put vpō hym his wyues raymēt ₮ went to the

herber and when he was gone thyder the prentys cã in to bed to his maistres wher for a seasõ they wer both contẽt ã pleasyd ech other by the space of
an hour or.ij. but when she thought tyme cõuenyẽt she sayd to the prentyse
Now go thy way in to the herber ã mete hym ã take a good waster in thy
hãd ã say thou dydys it but to pue whether I woldbe a good womã or no ã
reward hym as thou thynkyst best. This prentys doig after his maistres cõ
cell wẽt to the herber wher he founde his maister i his maistres appel ã sayd
A thou harlot art thou come hether/now I se well yf I wold be fals to my
maister thou woldest be a strõg hore but I had leuer thou wer hãgyd thã I
wold do hym so tratrrous a dede therfore I shall gyue the some punishment
as thou lyke an hore hast deseruyd/ã ther with lapt hi wel about the sholbs
ã bak ã gaue hym a dole or.iij.good strypys the maister selyng hym selfe sõ,
what to imart sayd pese wyllã myne own true good seruãt for godys sake
hold thy hãdys for I ã thi maister ã not thi maistres na hore qd he thou lyest
thou art but an harlot ã I dyd but to pue the/ã smote hi agayn Alas man
quod the maister I beleue the nomore for I am not she for I am thy maister
sele for I haue a berd and therwith he sparyd his hãd ã felt hys berd Alas
maister qd the prentys I crye you mercy.ã then the maister went vnto hys
wyfe ã she askyd hym how he had sped ã he ãswerd Iwis wyfe I haue bene
shrewdly betyn how be it I haue cause to be glad for I thanke god I haue
as trew a wyfe ã as trew a seruant as any man hath in englond.

¶By this tale ye may se that it is not wysdome for a man to be culyd
alway after hys wyues councell.


T fortunyd that in a market towne in the counte of Suffolk
there was a stage play i the which playe on callyd John adro
yns wich dwelyd i a nother vyllage ij.myle frõ thẽs playd the
deuyll. And whẽ the play was done this John ad.oryns i the
euenyng departyd fro the sayd market towne to go home to hys owne house
ã be cause he had there no chãge of clothige he went forth i hys deuylls apell
whiche i the way comyg homwardẽ thorow a waren of conys belõgyng
to a getylmã of the vyllage wher he hym selfe dwelt.at which tyme it fortunyd a prest a vicar of a church therby with ij or iij.other vnthryfty felowes
had brought with thẽ a dogs a hey ã a feret to thẽtẽt ther to get conis ã whẽ
the feret was in the yerth ã the hey set ouer the path way wheri thys John
adroyns shold com.this prest ã this other felowes saw hym com i the deuyls
raymẽt cõsyderig that they were i the deuyls serupse ã stelig of cones ã sup,
posynge it had ben the deuyll in dede for fere ran away.this John adroyns
i the deuyls raymẽt ã be cause it was sõwhat dark saw not the hey but wẽt
forth i hast ã stõblid therat ã fell down ã wyth the fall he had almost broke

But whē he was a lytyll recuuyd he lokyd vp ꝓ spyed it was a hay to thach
connys ꝓ lokyd further / ꝓ saw that they ran away for fere of hym / ꝓ saw a
horse tyed to a bush laden with connys whych they had taken / ꝓ he tode the
horse ꝓ the haye ꝓ lepe vpō the horse ꝓ rode to the gentylmannys place that
was lorde of the waren / to the entente to haue thanke for takynge suche a
pray. And when he cam / knokyd at the gatys. To whome anone one of the
gentylmannys seruauntys alkyd who was there / and sodeynly openyd the
gate / and assone as he perceyuyd hym in the deuyls rayment was sodenly
abashyd / and sparryd the dore agayn / ꝓ went in to his mayster / and sayd ꝓ
sware to hys mayster that the deuyll was at the gate / and wolde come in.
The gentylman heryng hym say so callyd another of hys seruauntys ꝓ bad
hym go to the gate to knowe who was there. This seconde seruaūt cam to
the gate durst not open it / but alkyd with lowd voyce who was there. thys
Iohn Andȝoyns in the deuyls apperell aꝼswerd with a hye voyce and sayd
Tell thy master I must nedys speke with hym or I go. This secōd seruaūt
heryng that answer suppolynge also it had bene the deuyll / went in agayn
to his master and sayd thus / mayster yt is the deuyll in dede that ys at the
gate / and sayth he must nedys speke with you or he go hens. The gentylmā
than began a lytyll to bathe and callyd the Teward of hys howse / whyche
was the wysyst seruaunt that he had and bad hym to go to the gate and to
bryn ge hym sure worde who was there. This steward be cause he thought
he wold se surely who was there came to the gate and lokyd thorow the chy
nys of the gate in dyuers placys / and saw well that yt was the deuyll and
sat vpon an horse and hangynge aboute the saddell on euery syde sawe the
cony heddys hengynge down / than he came to his mayster aferde in greate
haste and sayd / By goddys body yt is the deuyll in dede that is at the gate
syttyng vpon an horse laden all wyth conyllys / and by lykelyhede / he is com
for your soule purposely / and lakkyth but your soule / ꝓ yf he had your sowle
I wene he shold be gone. This gentylman thā merueiously abashyd callyd
vp his chapleyn / and made the holy candell to be lyght / and gat holy water
and wente to the gate wyth as many of hys seruauntys as durste go with
hym / where the chaplayn with holy wordys of coniuracyon sayde / In the
name of the fader / sonne and holy goost. I coniure the and charg the in the
holy name of god to tell me why and wherfore thowe commyste hyther.
This Iohn Andȝoynys in the deuyllys apparell heryng them begynne to
coniure after suche maner sayd / Nay nay be not aferd of me for I am a good
deuell I am Iohn Adroyns your neghbour dwellyng in thys towne and
he that played the deuyll to day in the play / I haue brought my mayster a
dosen or / ii. of hys owne conyes that were stolyn in hys waren and theyr
horse ꝓ theyr hay / and maꝛe them for fere to ronne away / and when they

herde hym thus speke by hys voyce they knew hym well ynoughe and ope=
nyd the gate and let hym come in/And so all the forsayd fere and dred was
tornyd to myrth and dysporte.

By this tale ye may se that mē fear many tymes moꝛe than they nede
which hath causyd mē to beleue that spyrytys ꝯ deuyls haue bene sene
in dyuers placys when it hath bene nothynge so•

Ther was a riche man which lay soꝛe seke in his bed lyke to dy wher
foꝛe hys eldyst son cam to hym ꝯ besechyd hym to gyue hym his blys
syng to whom the fader sayd son thou shalt haue goddys blessyng ꝯ myne/ꝯ
foꝛ that that thou hast ben euer good of cōdycyons I gyue ꝯ bequeth the all
my land/ to whom he answered ꝯ sayd nay sad I trust you shall lyue ꝯ occu
py them your selfe full well by goddys grace. Sone after came his ij. sone
to hym lyke wyse ꝯ desyred his blessyng/to whom the sad sayd because thou
hast be euer kynde ꝯ gentyll ꝯ I geue the goddys blessynge ꝯ myn and also
I bequeth the all my mouable goodys/to whom he answerd and sayd/nay
fader I trust ye shall lyue ꝯ do well ꝯ spend and vse your goodys your selfe
by goddys grace. Anon after the iij. sone cam to hym ꝯ desyred his blessyng
to whom the fader answerd ꝯ sayd by cause thou hast bene euyll ꝯ stoboꝛne
of condycyons ꝯ wolde neuer be ruled after my coūsell I haue nother land
noꝛ goodys onbequethyd but onely a lytell vacant ground wher a galows
standyth which now I geue and bequeth to the / and goddys curse withall
to whom the sonne answerd as hys bꝛethꝛne dyd ꝯ sayd nay fader I trust
ye shall lyue ꝯ be in good helth and haue yt and occupy it your selfe by god
dys grace. But after that the fader dyed ꝯ this thyꝛd son cōtynuyd styll hys
vnthꝛyfty condycyons wherefoꝛe yt was hys foꝛtune afterwarde foꝛ hys de
seruyng to be hangyd on the same galows

By this tale men may wel perceyue that yong people that wyll not be ru
lyd by theyꝛ frendys councell in youth in tymes come to a shamfull ende.

Two gētylmen of accoyntāce wer apportyd to ly witha geyll two
C ma in one nyght the one not knowige of the other at dyuers tymes
This fyꝛst ad his houre appoyntyd cā/ꝯ in the bed ther he foꝛtunid
to lese a ryng/the.ij.gentylmā when he was gone cam / ꝯ foꝛtunid to fynd
the same rynge ꝯ when he had sped hys besynes departyd, ꝯ.ij.oꝛ.iij.dayes
after the furst gētylman seyng his ryng on the others fynger chalengyd yt
of hym he ꝯ denyed yt hym ꝯ bad hi tell wher he had lost it ꝯ he seyd i such a
gentylwomans bed than quod the other ꝯ ther founde I yt. ꝯ the one sayd
he wolde haue yt/the other sayd he shulde not/thā they agreed to be iuggid
by the nert mā that they mete/ ꝯ it foꝛtunid theym to mete with the hulbād
of the sayd gentyll womā ꝯ desyrd hym of his best Jugemēt shewyng hym
all hole mater/then quod he by my iugemēt he that owd the ringys shuld ha
ue the ryng/thē quod they ꝯ foꝛ your good iugemēt you shall haue the ryng.

I Na vyllage in suſſex there dwellyd a huſbandmã whoſe wyfe
fortunyd to fall ſyk. ¶Thys huſbandman came to the preſt
of the church and deſyryd hys counceil what thyng was beſt to
help his wyfe/whych anſweryd hym ⁊ ſayd þ in bꝛeoſtrete in londõ there
was a connyng Phyſycyon whoſe name is callyd maſter Jordayne/Go
to hym ⁊ ſhew hym that thy wyfe is ſyk and Jmpotent ⁊ not able to go ⁊
ſhew hym her water and beſecch hym to be good maſter to the/and praye
hym to do hys cure vppon her:and J warrant he wyll tech the ſome med=
ſyne that ſhall help her.Thys huſbandman folowyng hys counceil cã to
london ⁊ aſkyd of dyuers men which was the way to good ale ſtrete ſo þ
euery man þ hard hym laught hym to ſcorne. At the laſt one þ harde hym
aſkyd him whether it were not bꝛed ſtrete that he wold haue/By god quod
the huſbandmã ye ſay treuth:for J wyſt well it was other bꝛede or dꝛink:
So whã they had taught hym the way to bꝛed ſtrete ⁊ was eteryd into þ
ſtrete he aſkyd of dyuers men where one maſter Pyſpot dwellyd whych
ſayd they knew no ſuch mã ⁊ laught at hym apace. At laſt one aſkyd him
whether it were not maſter Jordayn þ phyſyciõ. ye þ ſame quod þ huſband
mã for J wot well a Jordayn ⁊ a pyſpot is all one. So whã they had ſhe=
wyd hym hys houſe he wet thyder ⁊ cã to hym ⁊ dyd hys erãd thus ⁊ ſayd
Syr:if it pleaſe your maſhyp J vnderſtand ye ar callyd a conyng confu=
ſyon:So it is my wyfe is ſyk ⁊ omnypotent ⁊ may not go ⁊ here J haue
bꝛought you her water J beſech you do your corage vppon her ⁊ J ſhall
gyue your maſhyp a good reward.The phyſycõ pleꝑuyng by the water
þ ſhe was ſyke of nature bad hym get her mete þ were reſtoratyue ⁊ ſpe
cyally if he coud let her haue a poũdgarnet ⁊ to let her not ouercõme her
ſtomak wᵗ mych mete tyll ſhe haue an apetyte. Thys huſbãdmã herd hym
ſpeke of a poundgarnet ⁊ an apetite had wend he had ſpoken of a pound
of garlyk and of an ape ⁊ ſhoꝛtly bought a pound of garlyk ⁊after went
to the ſhypyard ⁊ hought an ape of one of the marchantꝭ ⁊ brought both
home to hys wyfe ⁊ tyed the ape wᵗ a cheyn at hys beddꝭ fete/⁊ made hys
wyfe to ete the pound of garlyk whether ſhe wolde oꝛ no/whereby ſhe fell
in ſo gret a laſk that it purgyd all the coꝛruptõ out of her body:wherby
⁊ by reſõ þ the ape that was tyde ther made ſo many mokkys ſkyppys ⁊
knakkꝭ that made her oftpyns to be mery ⁊ laugh that thankyd be god
ſhe was ſhoꝛtly reſtoryd to helth.

¶By thys tale ye may ſe that oft tymps medeſyns taken at ad=
uentureys do as mich good to the Pacyent as medeſyns geuen
by the ſolempne couicil of conyng phyſicyons.

.B.i.

IN the vnyuersyte of Oronforð there was a scoler ð delyteð
mich to speke eloquent englissh & curious termes/And ca to ð
cobler wyth hys shoys whych were pibið befor as they vseð ð
reson to haue them cloutyð & sayð thys wyse/Cobler I pray the let me...
rypangpls &.ii..semy cercles vppon my subpedytals & I shall gyue the lo?
thy labor/Thys cobler bccause he vnderstode hym not half well answerið
shortly & sayd/Syr youre eloquence passith myne itelligence/but I promyse you yf ye meddyll wyth me/the dowtyng of youre shone shall coste
you.iii. pence.

℘By thys tale me may lerne ð it is foly to study to speke eloquet-
ly before them that be rude & vnlernyð.

Certayn artificer in londo there was which was sore syk that
coud not well dygest hys mete/to whom a physytyon cam to gyue
hym councell & leyð ð he must vse to ete metis ð be light ot dygestyon as small byrdys/as sparous or swallous & especyall ð byrð ð ys
callyð a wagtayle whose tlesshe ys nutrytyue lyght of dygestyon becausc
that byrð ys euer mouyng & styryng. The lik man heryng the phesition
seyð so answeryð hym & seyd/Syr yf that be the cause ð those byrdys be
lyght of dygestyon Than I know a mete mychlyghter of dygestion tha
other sparow swallow or wagtayle/& that ys my wyuys tong for it is neuer in rest but euer mouyng & styryng.

℘By thys tale ye may lerne a good generall rule of physyk.

A woman ther was whych had had.iiii.husbond. It fortunyd also
that this fourth husband dieð & was broüht to chirch vppon ð
bere/who this woman folowyð & made gret mone & wext very sory. In so
mych that her neybours thought she wold sowne & dy for sorow/wherfor
one other gossyps cam to her & spake to her in her ere & bad her for goddes
sake to comfort her self & refrayne that lamentacon or ellys it wold hurt
her gretly & pauenture put her in ieopdy of her lyfe. To whom this woman
answeryð & sayd/I wys good gossyp I haue gret cause to morne if ye knew
all/for I haue byryeð.iii.husbandys besyde thys man/but I was neuer i
the case ð I am now/for there was not one of the but whe that I folowið
the corse to chyrch yet I was sure alway of an other husbad before that ð
corse cam out of my house/& now I am sure of no nother husband & ther
fore ye may be sure I haue gret cause to be sad & heuy.

℘By thys tale ye may se that the olde puerbe ys trew that yt is as
gret pyte to se a woman wepe as a gose to go bareiote.

A    Nother woman there was that knelyd at þ mas of requiē whyle
the corse of her husbande lay on the bere in the chyrch. To whom
a yonge man came to speke wyth her in her ere as thoughe hyt had bene
for som matter concernyng the funerallys / howe be yt he spake of no suche
matter but only wowyd her that he myghte be her husbande / to whome
the answeryde & sayde thus / Syr by my trouthe I am sory that ye come
so late / for I am sped all redy / For I was made sure yester day to a nother man.

⁋ By thys tale ye maye perceyue that women ofte tymes be wyse and
lothe to lose any tyme.

A    Merchant that thought to deride a mylner seyd vnto þ mylner
syttyng among company. Sir I haue hard say that euery trew
mylner that tollyth trewlye hath a gyldeyn thombe / the mylner answe
red & seyd it was trewth / Then quod the merchaunt I pray the let me se
thy thomb / & when the mylner shewyd hys thomb. the merchaunt sayd I
can not perceyue þ thy thombe is gylt / but yt ys but as all other mennys
thōbis be / to whom the mylner answeryd & seyd / Syr tre wthe yt ys that
my thōb is gylt how be it ye haue no power to se it / for ther is a properte
euer incidēt therto þ he þ ys a cokecold shall neuer haue power to se yt.

O    Ne callyd Oconer an yrish lorde toke an horseman prysoner that
was one of hys grete ennmys / whiche for any request or yntretyp þ þ
horsman made gaue iugement that he shulde incōtynēt be hāgyd / & made a frere to shryue hym and bad hym make hym redy to dye. Thys frere
þ shroue hym examyned hym of dyuers synes & askyd hym amōg othere
whyche were the grettyste synnys that euer he dyde / thys horsemanc answeryd & sayde one of the grettyst actys that euer I dyde whyche I now
most repent is that when I toke Oconer the laste weke in a churche and
ther I myght haue brennyd hym church and all & because I had conscyen
ce & pyte of brennyng of the church I taryed þ tyme so long þ oconer esca
ped / & that same deferring of brennyng of the chirch & so long taryeng of
that tyme is one of the worst actys þ euer I dyd wherof I moste repente /
Thys frere perceyuyng hym in that mynd sayd pece man in the name of
god & change þ mynde & dye in charite or els thou shalt neuer come in heuen / nay quod the hors man I wyll neuer change þ mynde what so euer
shall come to my soule / thys frere preyuyng hym thus styll to contynew
hys mide cā to oconer & seyd syr in þ name of god haue some pyte vppō
thys mannys sowle & let hym not dye now tyll he be in a better mynde /

.B.ii.

For yf he dye now he hys so far out of charyte ẏ ѵtterly hys soule shalle be
dampnyd /and she wyd hym what mynde he was in ꝺ all the hole matter
as ys before shewyd. Thys horsman heryng ẏ frere thus intrete for hym
sayd to oroner thus / Oroner thou seeyst well by thys mannys reporte ẏ
yf I dye now I am out of charyte ꝺ not redy to go to heuen / ꝺ so it ys ẏ I
am now out of charyte in dede / but thou seest well ẏ this frere ys a good
man he is now well dysposyd ꝺ in charyte / and he is redy to ɡo to heuen
ꝺ so am not I / therfore I pray the hang vp thys frere whyle that he hys
redy to go to heuyn and lette me tary tyl a nother tyme ẏ I may be i char
ryte and redy ꝺ mete to go to heuyn. This Oroner heryng this mad an
swere of hym spatyd the man ꝺ forgaue hym hys lyfe at that season.

By thys ye may se that he that is in daunger of hys enmye ẏ hath
no pyte / he can do no better than shew to hym the vttermoste of hys
malycyous mynde whych that he beryth toward hym.

He archbckyn of Essex ẏ had bene long in auctoryte in a tyme
ꝺ of vysytacion when all the preestys apperyd before hym callyd
before .iii. of ẏ yong preestys whych were accusyd ẏ they coud not
well say theyr breuyne seruyce / ꝺ askyd of the whe they sayd mas whether
they sayd corpus meus or corpu meu. The furst preest sayd ẏ he sayd cor
pus meus. The secod sayd ẏ he sayd corpu meu. And the he askyd of the
thyrd how he sayd / whych aunweryd ꝺ sayd thus / lyn because it is so gret
a dout ꝺ dyuere men be in dyuers opynyons / therfore because I wold be
sure I wold not offend whe I come to ẏ place I leue it clene out ꝺ say no
thyng therfore / wherfore he then openly rebukyd them all thre. But dy
uers that were present thought more defaut in hym because he hym seue
before tyme had admytryd them to be preestys.

By thys tale ye may se that one ought to take hede how he rebu
kyth an other lest it torne most to hys owne rebuke.

Two frerys sat at a gentylmans tabyll whych had before hym ꝺ
a fastyngday an ele ꝺ cut the hed of the ele ꝺ layd it vppo one of
ẏ frer trechars / but the frere because he wold haue had of ẏ
myddyll part of the ele sayd to the gentylman he louyd no ele heddꝭ / this
gentylman also cut the tayle of ẏ ele ꝺ leyd it on the other frer trechar /
he lykewyse because he wold haue had of the myddyll pte of ẏ ele sayd he
louyd no ele taylys. Thys gentylma perceyuing that / gaue the tayle to
the frere ẏ sayd he leuyd not the hed / ꝺ gaue the hed to hym that sayd he
louys not ẏ tayle. And as for the myddyll parte of the ele he ete part hym

felf ꝫ part he gaue to other folke at ꝑ table/wherfore thefe fretes for au
ger wold ete neuer a mossell/ꝫ so they for all theyr craft ꝫ subtylte were
not onely deceyued of ꝑ best mossell of ꝑ ele/but therof had no part at al.
¶By this ye se that they ꝑ couet the best part somtyme therfore
lose the meane part and all.

A welchman dwellynge in a wylde place of walys came to hys
curate in the tyme of lent ꝫ was cōfessyd. ꝫ when his confessyon
was in maner at the end the curate asked him whether he had any other
thyng to say ꝑ greuyd hys cōscyēce/whych sore abasshyd answeryd no
word a gret whyle/at last by exortacion of hys goostly fader he sayd ꝑ
there was one thyng in his mynd that gretly greuyd hys cōsciēce whic̄
he was ashamed to vtter/for it was so greuous ꝑ ye trowid god wold
neuer forgyue hym/to whom the curate aswered ꝫ sayd ꝑ goddꝭ mercy
was aboue all/ꝫ bad hym not dyspayre in the mercy of god/for what so
euer it was yf he were repentaute ꝑ god wold forgyue hym/And so by
long exortacion at the last he shewyd it ꝫ seyd thus /Syr it happenyd
onis that as my wyfe was makinge a chese vppon a fryday I wold haue
sayd whether it had ben salt or freth and toke a lytyll of the whey in my
hand ꝫ put it in my mouth ꝫ or I was ware part of it went downe my
throte agaynst my wyll ꝫ so I brake my fast/to whom the curate sayd ꝫ if
ther be no nother thyng I warant god shall forgyue the. So whā he had
well comfortyd hym w̄ ꝑ mercy of god the curate prayd hym to answer a
question ꝫ to tell hym treuth/ꝫ when the welchman had promysyd to tell
the treuth/the curate sayd that there were robberys ꝫ murders done nye
the place where he dwelt ꝫ dyuers men foūd slayne ꝫ askyd hym whether
he were cōsentyng to any of them /to whō he answerid ꝫ seyd yes ꝫ sayd
he was ꝑtee to many of them ꝫ dyd helpe to robbe ꝫ to sle dyuers of them
¶Then the curate askyd hym why he dyd not cōfesse him therof/the welch
man aswered ꝫ sayd he toke ꝑ for no synne for it was a custome amonge
them ꝑ whan any boty came of any ryche merchaunt rydyng ꝑ it was but
a good neyghbours dede one to help a nother when one callyd a nother/ꝫ
so they toke that but for good felyshyp ꝫ neybourhod.

¶Here ye may se ꝑ some haue remorse of conscyence of small venyall
synys ꝫ fere not to do gret offenc̄ wout shame of ꝑ world or drede of
god :ꝫ as ꝑ cōen prouerb is they stūble at a straw ꝫ lepe ouer a blok.

¶ A ryche couetous marchāte ther was ꝑ dwellyd in Lōdon whych
euer gaderyd money ꝫ coud neuer fynd in hys hert to spend no
ght vppon hym self nor vppon no mā els/whych fell sore syk/ꝫ as he lay

on hys deth) bed had hys purs lyeng at his beddys hed/ꝛ had suche a loue
to hys money that he put his hand in his puꝛs ꝛ toke out therof. x. oꝛ. xii. li
i nobles ꝛ put them in his mouth/And becaule his wyfe ꝛ other peeꝛuyꝺ
hym very lyk ꝛ lyke to dye they croꝛtyꝺ hym to be conteffyꝺ and bꝛought
ꝑ curate vnto hym/whych when they had caulyꝺ hym to ley Benedicite ꝑ
curat bad hym cry god mercy ꝛ ꝺhew his fynnys. Than this fyk man be=
gan to ley I cry god mercy I haue offenꝺyꝺ in ꝑ. vij. ꝺeꝺly fynnys ꝛ bꝛo=
ken the. x. commaunꝺementys/ꝛ becaule of the gold in hys mouth he muf=
flede fo in hys fpeche that the curate cowꝺe not well vnꝺerftanꝺe hym/
wherefoꝛe the curate afkeꝺ hym what he haꝺꝺe in hys mouthe that letteꝺ
hys fpeche / I wys maftere perfone quoꝺ the fyk man muffelynge I haue
nothyng in my mouth but a lyttyll money becaule I wot not whether I
ꝺhall go I thoughte, I wolꝺe take fome fpenꝺyng money wyth me foꝛ I
wot not what neꝺe I ꝺhall haue therof/ And incontynent after that ley
ꝛynge ꝺyeꝺ befoꝛe he was confeffeꝺ oꝛ repentant that ony man coulꝺ per
ceue/and fo by lyklyhoꝺe went to the deuyll.

By thys tale ye may fe that they that all theyꝛe lpuys wylle neuer ꝺo
charyte to theyꝛ neyghbours/that goꝺ in tyme of theyꝛ ꝺethe wyll not
fuffer them to haue gꝛace of repentaunce.

Here was a certayn ryche hufbanꝺman in a vyllage whych loueꝺ
nottes merueloufly well ꝛ fet trees of filberꝺys ꝛ other nut trees
in his oꝛchaꝛꝺ/ꝛ norꝛ ꝺhiꝺ them well all hys lyfe/ꝛ when he ꝺyeꝺ he maꝺe
hys executours to make pꝛomife to bery wt hym yn hys graue a bage of
nottis oꝛ els they ꝺholꝺe not be hys executours/which executours foꝛ fe=
re of lofyng theyꝛe roinys fulfyllyꝺ hys wyll ꝛ ꝺyꝺ fo. It happenyꝺ ꝑ the
fame nyght after that he was beryeꝺ there was a ii. ylnere in a whyte co=
te came to this mays garꝺen to theter to ftele a bag of nottis/ꝛ in ꝑ way
he met wt a tayler in a blak cote an vnthꝛift of hys accoyntaüce ꝛ ꝺhewyꝺ
hym hys intent. This tayler lyke wyfe ꝺhewyꝺ hym ꝑ he inteꝺyꝺ ꝑ fame
tyme to ftele a ꝺhepe/ꝛ fo they both there agreyꝺ to go foꝛthwarꝺ euery
man feuerally wt hys purpofe ꝛ after ꝑ they apoyntyꝺ to make good che=
re eel wt other ꝛ to mere agayne in ꝑ chyꝛch porch/ꝛ he that came furft to
tary foꝛ the other This mylner when he haꝺ fpeꝺe of hys nottys came
furft to the chyꝛch porche ꝛ there taryeꝺ foꝛ hys felowe anꝺ the mene why
le fatte ftyll there ꝛ knakkeꝺ nottys. It foꝛtuneꝺ than the ferten of the
church becaule yt was abowt. ix. of the clok cam to ꝛyng curfu. ꝛ when he

lokyd in þ porch ꝯ faw one all in whyte knakkyng nott⁊/he had went
it had bene þ dede man rylen owt of hys graue knakkynge þ nottes þ
wer bycryed whyin ꝯ ran home agayn in all haſt and tolde to a krepyll þ
was in hys howle what he had ſene. This erepyll thus heryng rebu
kyd þ ſerten ꝯ ſeyd þ yf he were able to go he wold go thyder ꝯ coture þ
ſprite/by my trouth qð þ ſerte ꝯ yf thou darſt do þ J wyl bere the on my
nek ꝯ ſo they both agreo. The ſerten toke þ erepull on hys nek ꝯ cam in
to þ chyrchyaro agayn/ꝯ þ mylner in þ porch ſaw one comyng bering
a thing on his bak had went it had ben þ taylour comyng w the ſhepe
ꝯ roſe vp to mete the⁊ꝯ as he cam towaroe the he aſkeyd ꝯ ſeyd/ Js he
fat/is he fat/þ ſerten heryng hym ſey ſo/for fere caſt the erepull down ꝯ
ſeyd fat or lene take hym ther for me/ꝯ ran away / ꝯ the creple by myra
cle was made hole. ꝯ ran away as faſt as he or faſter. This mylner per
ceyuing þ they were. ii. ꝯ þ one ran after a nother ſuppoſyng þ one had
ſpyed þ tayler ſtelyng þ ſhepe and þ he had ron after hym to haue taken
hym/and tered þ ſom booy alſo had ſpyed hym ſtelyng nottes he for fe
re left hys nottes behynd hym and as ſecretly as he cowde ran home to
hys myll/ And anon after þ he was gon þ tayler cam w the ſtolyn ſhepe
vpon hys nek to the cyrreh porch to ſeke the mylner ꝯ when he fownd
ther the not ſharp he ſuppoſed þ hys felow had be ther and gone home
as he was in oeoe/wherefore he toke vp þ ſhepe agayne on hys nek and
went toward the myl/ But yet duryng this whyle the ſerte whych ran
away went not to hys owne houſe but wet to the pryſh prytis chaoer/ꝯ
ſhewd hym how the ſpryte of þ man was ryſe out of hys graue knakkig
nottes as ye haue haro before/wherfor þ preſt ſayd that he wold go cou
re hym yf the ſerten wold go w hym /ꝯ ſo they both agreed/þ preſt dyd
on his ſurples ꝯ a ſtole aboue hys nek ꝯ toke holy water w hym and cam
w the ſerte toward þ church /ꝯ as ſone as he enteryd in to þ church yat
de /The tayler w the whyte ſhepe on hys nek intendyng as J before ha
ue ſhewid yow to go down to þ myll met w them ꝯ had went þ þ preſt in
hys ſurples had ben þ mylner in hys whyte core /ꝯ ſeyd to hym by god
J haue hym J haue hym meanyng by the ſhepe þ he had ſtolyn/the preſt
perceyuynge the tayler all in biak ꝯ a whyte thyng on hys nek had went
it had ben þ deuyll bcryng away the ſpryte of þ deoe man þ was beryed
ꝯ ran away as faſte as he coud takyng þ way downe toward the myl/ꝯ
þ ſerten ronnyng after hi. This tayler ſeyng one folowyng hi had wet
þ one had folowed the mylner to haue don hym ſome hurt ꝯ thought he
wold folow if nede were to help þ mylner. ꝯ went forth til he cam to the
myl ꝯ knokked at þ myldore/þ mylner beyng wyn aſked who was ther
þ tayler aſwerd ꝯ ſaid by god J haue caught one of them ꝯ made hi ſure

& tyed hym fast by þ leggys meuynge by the ſhepe þ he had ſtolyn & had the on hys nck tyed faſt by þ leggys. But þ mylner heryng hym ſey þ he had hym tyed faſt by the leggys had wente it had bē the conſtable þ had take the tayler foꝛ ſtelyng of the ſhepe & had tyed hym by þ legge / & tend þ he had comē to haue takē hym alſo to: ſtelyng of the noteys / wherfo ꝛe the mylner openyd a bak doꝛe & ran away as faſt as he coud. The tay= lour heryng the bak doꝛe openyng wēt on þ other ſyde of þ myll / & there ſaw the mylner ronnyng away / & ſtode there a lyttyll whyle muſyng wᵗ þ ſhepe on his nck. Then was the paryſh preeſt & the ſexte ſtandyng there vnder the myllhouſe hydyng thēin foꝛ tere & ſaw the taylour agayn wᵗ þ ſhepe on his nck had wend ſtyll it had bene the dyuyll wᵗ the ſpyꝛyt of the dede man on hys nck & foꝛ fere ran away / but becauſe they knew not the ground well / the preeſt lepte into a dyche almoſt ouer the hed lyke to be dꝛounyd that he cryed wyth a loud voyce help help. Then the taylour lo kyd about & ſaw the mylner rōne away & the ſexten a nother way & hard the preeſt cry help: had wend it had bene the cōſtable wᵗ a gꝛet cōpany cry eng foꝛ help to take hym & to bꝛyng hym to pꝛyſon foꝛ ſtelyng of þ ſhepe wherfoꝛe he threw downe the ſhepe & ran away a nother way as faſte as he coud / & ſo euery man was afred of other wythout cauſe.

⸿By thys ye may ſe well it is foly foꝛ any man to fere a thyng to nygh tyll that he ſe ſome pꝛoue oꝛ cauſe.

Ꝑ þ old woꝛld when all thyng coud ſpeke þ .iiii. elementꝭ met to geder foꝛ many thyngꝭ whych they had to do becauſe they muſt meddyll alway one wᵗ a nother: & had cōmunicaciō to geder of dyuers matters / & becauſe they coud not conclude all theyꝛ ma= ters at þ ſeaſon they appoyntyd to bꝛeke comunycacyon foꝛ þ tyme & to mete agayn a nother tyme / therfoꝛe erh one of thē ſhewyd to other wher theyꝛe moſt abydyng was & where theyꝛ felowes ſhuld fynd thē if nede ſhuld requyꝛe: & fyrſt þ erth ſayd bꝛethern ye know well as foꝛ me I am pmanēt alway & not remouable therfoꝛ ye may be ſure to haue me alway whan ye lyſt. The water ſeyd yf ye lyſte to ſeke me ye ſhalbe ſure euer to haue me vnder a roſt of grene ruſſhys oꝛ clyps in a womans eye. The wynde ſayd yf ye lyſt to ſeke me ye ſhalbe ſure euer to haue me amonge aſpyn leuys oꝛ els in a womans tong. Then quod the fyꝛe yf any of you lyſt to ſeke me: ye ſhall euer be ſure to fynd me in a flynt ſtone oꝛ els in a womans hart.

⸿By thys tale ye may lerne aſwell the pꝛopertes of þ .iiii. elemen= tys as the pꝛoperte of a woman.

Here was a iustyce but late in ꝑ realme of englond called master
Hauysour a very homly man & rude of condycions & louyd ne=
uer to spēd mych money / This master Hauysour rode on a tyme in hys
cyrcute in a place of the north cōtrey where he had agreed wt the shyryf
for a certayn some of money for hys chargys thorowe the shyre / so that
at euery Inne & lodgyng thys master Hauesour payd for hys own collys
It fortunyd so ꝑ when he cam to a certayn lodgyng he cōmaunded one
Torpyn hys seruāt to se ꝑ he vsed good husbondry & to saue suche thyn
ges as were laft & to cary it wt hym to serue hym at the next baytyng /
Thys Torpyn doyng hys masters cō̄maudemēt toke ꝑ brokyn brede
brokyn mete & all (sych) thig ꝑ was laft & put it in hys male / The wyfe
of ꝑ house perceyuyng ꝑ he toke all suche fragmentys & vptayle wt hym ꝑ
was laft & put it in hys male / she brought vp ꝑ podege ꝑ was laft i the
pot & when torpyn had tornyd hys bak a lytyll syde she pouryd ꝑ pode
ge in to ꝑ male whych ran vpon hys robe of skarlet & other hys garmē=
tys & rayed them very euyll that they were mych hurt therwt. Thys Tor
pyn sodeynly tornyd him & saw it / reuylyd the wyfe therfor & ran to hys
master & told hym what she had don / wherfor master Hauesour incōt
nēt callyd ꝑ wyfe & seyd to her thus. Thou drab qꝑ he what hast thou dō
why hast thou pouryd ꝑ podege in my male & marryd my raymēt & gere /
O syr quod ꝑ wyfe I know well ye ar a iudge of ꝑ realme / & I perceyue
by you : your mid is to do ryght & to haue that that is your owne / & your
mynd is to haue all thyng wt you ꝑ ye haue payd for / both brokyn brede
mete & other thyng ꝑ is left : & so it is reason that ye haue / & therfore be=
cause your seruant hath taken the brede & the mete & put it i your male I
haue therfore put in your male the podege ꝑ be laft because ye haue well
& truly payd for them for yt I shuld kepe ony thyng from you ꝑ ye haue
payd for : peraduenture ye wold troble me in the law an other tyme.

Here ye may se ꝑ he ꝑ playth the nygarde to mych sometyme yt
torneth hym to hys owne losse.

Certayne weddyd man there was whyche whan he was dede
cā to heuen gatys to saynt Peter & saydhe cā to claym his he
rytage which he had deseruyd. Seynt Peter askyd hym what
he was / & he sayd a weddyd mā / anon Seynt peter openyd ꝑ gate & bad
hym come in & sayd he was worthy to haue hys herytage because he had
had much trobyll & was worthy to haue a crowne of glory. Anon after ꝑ
there cam a nother man that claymyd heuyn & sayd to Seynt Peter he
had had. ii. wyuys / to whom Seynt peter āsweryd and sayd come in for
thou art worthy to haue a doble crown of glory / for thou hast had doble
troble / at ꝑ last there cam a thyrd claymyng heuen & sayd to Saynt peter

þ he had had .iii. wyurs ⁊ defyꝛyd to colne in/what quod Seynte Peter
thou haſt bene vnys in troble ⁊ therof delpuerpd/⁊ then wyllyngly wol
dyſt be tꝛobyld agayn ⁊ yet agayn therof delpuerpd/⁊ foꝛ all þ couldꝭ not
beware þ thy delpyne/but entereſt wyllyngely in trobyll agayne there
foꝛe go thy way to hell foꝛ thou ſhalte neuer come in heuen foꝛ thou arte
not woꝛthy.

℟ Thys tale is a warnyng to them that houe bene twyſe in parell
to beware how they come therin the thyꝛd tyme.

A Rych merchant of londou there was which had but one fonne
þ was fomewhat vnthꝛyfty therfoꝛe his faoer vppon hys deth
bed called hym to hyꝝ ⁊ ſeyd he knew well þhe had ben vnthꝛif
ty howbeyt yf he knew he wold amend hys condiciõs i.e wold make hym
his executoure ⁊ leue hꝝ in his goodys to þ he wold pꝛompte to pꝛaye foꝛ
hys fowle: ⁊ to fynde one dayly to ſyng foꝛ hꝝ in/whꝛche tyyng to perfoꝛ
me hys fon there made a faythfull pꝛompfe. After þ thys in̄ made hym
hys executoure ⁊ dyed/But after that hys fône kept luthꝛyot þ in ſhoꝛt
tyme he had waſted ⁊ ſpend all ⁊ had nothꝝ uge left but a hen ⁊ a cok that
was hys faders. It foꝛtunyd than that one of hys frendys came to hym
⁊ ſayd he was foꝛy þ he had waſtyd ſo myꝛh ⁊ alſo þe hꝝ in how he wolde
pfomn hys pmyfe made to hys father þ he wold kepe one to ſing foꝛ hym
℟ Thys yong man afweryd ⁊ ſayd by god yet I wyll perfoꝛme my pꝛo
myfe/foꝛ I wyll kepe thys fame cok alyue ſtyll and he wyll krowe euery
daye and fo he ſhall fynge euery day foꝛ my faders fowle/⁊ fo I wyll per
foꝛme my pꝛompfe well ynough.

℟ By thys ye may fe that it is wyſtome foꝛ men to do good
dedys hym felf whyle he is here ⁊ not to truſt to the prayer and
pꝛomys of hys executours.

T Here was a mayde ſtode by a ryuers ſyde in her fmok waſhynge
clothys. And as ſhe ſtoupyd oft tymys her fmokke cleuyd v
twene her butokkes/By whome there came a trere ſeynge her and ſayd
in fpoꝛt. Mayd mayde take hede foꝛ Bayard bytys on the bꝛydyll. Nay
wyp maſter frere quod the mayden he doth but wype hys mouth and wc
nych ye wyll come ⁊ kyſſe hym.

℟ By thys ye may fe that a womans anſwer is neuer tofete.

Certayn man there was dwellynge in a towne callyd Gotam
which went to a fayre.iii.myle of to by shepe/ꞇ as he cam ouer
a brydge he met w one of hys neybours ꞇ told him whether he
went/ꞇ he askyd hym whych way he wold bryng the/whych sayd he wold
bꞟig the ouer the same brydge/nay quod the other man but thou shalt not
by god qd he but I wyll/ꝑ other agayn said he shuld not/ꞇ he agayn said
he wold bryng them ouer ſpyte of his teth ꞇ so fell at word/ꞇ at the last
to buffett that eche one knokkyd other well about the heddys w theyꞟe
fyſtys. To whom there cam a thyrd man which was a myner wyth a ſak
of mele vppon a horſe a neybour of theyꞟs ꞇ partyd them ꞇ askyd the what
was the cauſe of theyꞟ baryaunce/whych then ſhewyd hym the matter ꞇ
cauſe as ye haue harde/ Thys thyrd man the myner thought to rebuke
theyꞟ folyſhnes wyth a fayrlyer example ꞇ toke hys ſak of mele from his
hors bak ꞇ openyd it ꞇ pouryd all the mele in the ſak ouer the brydge into
the ronyng ryuer wherby all the mele was loſt ꞇ ſayd thus. By my trouth
neybors becauſe ye ſtryue for ojpuyng ouer the brydge thoſe ſhepe whych
be not yet bought noꞟ wot not where they be/me thynkyth therfore there
is euyn as mych wyt in your heddys as there is mele in my ſak.

**¶** Thys tale ſhewyth you that ſome man takyth vppon hym to
ſhew other men wyſdome when he is but a foic hym ſelf.


man there man that came to confeſſe hym ſelf to a gray frere ꞇ
ſhroue hym that he had layne wyth a yong gentilwoman ꝑ frere
than aſkyd hym in what place/the ſaid it was in a goouly chā
ber all nyght lōg in a ſoite warme bed/ The frere heryng that ſhꞟuggyd
in hꞟs clothꞟys ꞇ ſayd/now by ſwete ſeynt fraunces then waſt thou verye
well at eaſe.


Chandeler beig a wydower dwellig at holboꞟne bꞟige inlōdō
had a fayꞟe doughter/whom a yōg gentylman of dauys Jnne
woyd gꞟetly to haue hys pleaſure of her/whych by long ſute to
her made at ꝑ laſt grauntyd him ꞇ poyntyd hym to cōe vppon a night to her
faders houſe in ꝑ euenyng ꞇ ſhe wold conuey hym into her chāber ſecretly
whych was an inner chamber wythin her faders chāber. So accoꞟdig to
ꝑ poitmēt all thig was pfoꞟmyd ſo ꝑ he lay w her all nyght ꞇ made good
there tyll about.iiii.a cōk i ꝑ moꞟnig/at whych time it foꞟtunyd this yōg
gētylmā fell a coughig/whych cā vppō hym ſo ſoꞟe ꝑ he coud not reſtrayn

This yong wench then seeing her fader that lay in the next chamber had
him go put his hed in the draught lest þ her fader should here him:which
after her councell rose in his shyrt & so dyd / but then because of the sauor
of the draught it causyd him to cough much more & louder that þ wench is
fader hard him & askyd of his doughter what man was that þ coughid i
her chamber/she answeryd & sayd no body. But euer this yong man coughid
styll more & more whom the fader heryng seyd/by goddꝭ body hore thou
lyest I wyll se who lys there & rose out of ups bed: ¶The wench perceyuyng her fader rysyng cam to the gentylman & sayd take hede spz to your
selfe my fader cometh. ¶This gentylman sore therewith abashyd wolde
haue pullyd his hed out of the draught hole whych was very strayte for
his hed that he pullyd the sege bord vp therewyth/& hangyng about his
neck ran vppon the fader beyng an old man & gaue him a gret fall/& bare
him down & hurt his arme/& opyn yd the dorys & ran into þ strete wyth þ
draught borde about his neck toward Paups Inne as fast as he coud.
¶This wench for fere ran out of her senses & ouer & cd not there a moneth after. This gentylman as he ran vppon holborne brydge met wd a colyers
cart laden wd colys where there was .ii. or .iii. sextyⁿ horsys/which when
they saw this gentylman comyng start asyde & threw down þ cart wyth
colys/& drew it asyde & brake þ cart rope/wherby the colys tell out some
in one place some in an other/& after the horsys brake they trasys & ran
some toward smythfeld & some toward newgate that the colyer ran after
them & was & howre & more or he coud get his horse to geder agayn/By
whych tyme the people of the strete were rysen and cd to þ strete & saw yt
strawyd wyth colys euery onc for his part gaderyd vp the colys:that þ
most part of the colys were gone or the colyer had got his horsys. ¶But
duryng this whyle the gentylman wd thorow feynt andrews churchyard
toward Paups Inne/& there met wyth the sexte comyng to church to ryg
to morow mas:whych when he saw the gentylman in the churchyarde in
his shyrt wd the draght bord about his neck/had wend it had bene a spryt
& cryed alas alas & ran bak agayn to his house almost at þ partys
& for fere was almost out of his wyt þ he was þ worse halfe a yere after.
¶This gentilman than because Paups Inne gatys were not open went
on the bak syde & lept ouer the garden wall/but in lepyng the sege bord
so trobled him that he fell down in to the garden & had almost broke his
neck & there ley styll tyll þ the pryncipall cam in to the garden/whych when
he saw him ly there had wend some man had be slayne & there cast ouer þ
wall & durst not come nye him tyll he had callyd vp his company/whych
when many of the gentylmen wer come to gether/lokyd well vppon him
and knew him & after releuyd him/But the borde þ was about his neck

cauſyd his hed ſo to ſwell that they coud not get it of tyll they were fayne to cutte it of with hatchettys. Thus was the wench well lappyd/ ⁊ for fere ſhe ran frō her fader/her fads armewas hurt the colyar loſt his colys the ſexte was almoſt out of his wyt/⁊ the gentylman had almoſt broke his nek

A marchantys wyfe ther was in bowe paryſh in london ſome what ſtept in age to whō her mayd cam on a ſonday in lent after dyner ⁊ ſayd mayſtres quod ſhe they ryng at ſaynt Thomas of acres for ther ſhall be a ſermō preched anon/to whom the mayſtres anſwerd ⁊ ſayd mary god dys blyſſyng on thy hart for warnyng me therof ⁊ becauſe I ſlept not wel all this nyght I pray the brynge my ſtole with me for I wyll go thyder to loke whether I can take a nap there whyle the preſt is prechyng

By this ye may ſe that many on goth to churche as moche for other thyngys as for deuocyon.

Her was a certayn company of women gathered to geder in comunycacyon one happenyd thus to ſay her pygges after they were ſarowyd dyed and wolde not lyue and one olde wyfe of her accoyntance heryng her ſay ſo bad her get a cockoldys hat and put the pyggys therin ⁊ whyle after they were ſarowyd and they ſholde lyue/whych wyfe inten dyng to do after her counſell came to one of her goſſyppys and ſhewyd her what medecyne was thaugh her for her pyggys ⁊ prayd her to lend her her huſbandys hat/whych anſwerd her angerly and ſayd I wold thou knew yſt it Drabbe I haue none for my huſbande is no cookold for I am a good woman and ſo lyke wyfe euery wyfe anſwerd her in lyke maner that ſhe departyd frome many of them in anger and ſkoldynge. But whan ſhe ſawe ſhe coude get none ſhe came agayne to her goſſyppys all angerly and ſayd I haue gone round aboute to borow a cookoldys hat and I can get none wherefore yf I lyue another yere I wyll haue one of myn own and be out of my neyghbours daunger

By this tale a man may lerne that it is more wyſdome for a man to truſt more to his owne ſtore than to his neyghbours gentylnes.

Gentylman ⁊ a gentylwoman ſat togeder talkyn whiche gen tylman had gret payn in one of his teth.⁊ hapnyd to ſay to the gentylwoman thus. Ioys maſtres I haue a toth i my hed which greueth me very ſore wherfore I wold yt were in your tayle. She heryng hym ſayng ſo, anſwerd thus. In good fayth ſyr yf your toth were in my tale it coud do yt but lytyll good/but yf there be any thynge in my tale that can do your toth good I wold yt were in your teth.

By this ye may ſe that a womans anſwer is ſeldome to ſeke.

C i.

IN the tyme of lent a welchman cam to be confessyd of hys curat whych in hys cofessyon sayd that he had kyllyd a frere / to whom the curat sayd he coude not assoyle hym / yes qd the welchmã yf thou knewest all thou woldyst assoyle me well inough / & when the curat had comandyd hym to shew hym all the case he sayd thus mary ther wer .ii. freers & I myght haue slayn them both yf I had lyst but I let the one skape ther fore master curat set the tone agaynst the tother & then the offence ys not so great but ye may assoyle me well ynough.

¶ By this ye may se that dyuers menne haue so cupll & large cofey ens that they thynke yf they do one good dede or refrayne from the doynge of one cupll synne that yt ys a satysfaccyon for other synnes and offences.

¶Here was a company of getylmen in northãtonshyre whych went to hunte for deere in the porlewos in the gollet besyde stony strat ford / Among which gentylmen ther was one whych had a walche man to hys seruaunte a good archer / whiche when they came to a place where they thought they shold haue game / they made a ston dyng and poyntyd thys welchman to stand by a tre nygh the hye way and bad hym in any wyse to take hede that he shot at no raskall nor medle nat with out it were a male & yf it were a male to spare not / wel qd this welch man let me alone. And whan this walchman had stande there a whyle he sawe moche dere comynge / as well of Juntelere as of Raskall / but euer he let them go and toke no hede to theym. ¶And within an howre after he saw come rydyng in the hye way a man of the countrey whych had a boget hangynge at his sadyll bowe. And whan this walche man had espyed hym he bad hym stand & began to drawe his bow and bad hym deliuer that lyt tyll male that hynge at his sadell bowe / Thys man for fere of his lyfe was glad to delyuer hym his boget / & so dyd & than rode his way & was glad he was so escapyd. And whan this man of the countrey was gon thys welch man was very glad & went incontynient to seke his master & at last founde hym with his company / and whã he sawe hym he come to hym & sayd thus Master by cottys plut & her naple I haue stande yonder thys two howrys and I cowd se neuer a male but a lytell male that a man had hangyng at his sadell bow / & that I haue gotten / lo here it is / and toke his master the boget whych he had taken awey from the forsayd man / for the whyche dede bothe the master & the seruant were afterwarde in great trouble.

¶ By thys ye may lerne yt ys gret foly for a master to put a seruaut to that besynes wherof he can nothyng skyll and wherin he hath nat be vsyd.

yonge gentylman of the age of.rr.yere fome whate dyfpofyd to
myrth and game on a tyme talkyd with a gentylwoman which
was ryght wyfe and alfo mery.this gentyll woman as fhe tal=
kyd with hym happenyd to loke vppon hys berde / whiche was
but yong and growen fome what vppon the ouer lyppe and but
lyttyll growen beneth as all yonge mennys berdys cōmonly vfe to growe
fayd to hym thus.Syr ye haue a berde aboue and none beneth. and he he=
ryng her fay fo/fayd in fporte/maftres ye haue a berde benethe and none
aboue/mary quod fhe/then fet the tone agaynft the tother/which anfwere
made the gentylman fo abafhyd that he had not one worde to anfwer.

Here was a certayn white frere which was a very glotton and
a great nyggyn whyche had an vngracyoufe boy that euer folo=
wyd hym and bare hys cloke/and what for the frerys glottony &
for his chorlyfhnes the boy where he went coulde fkant get mete
inough for the frere wolde eet almofte all hym felfe. But on
a tyme the frere made a fermon in the cōtrey wherin he touchyde very ma=
ny myracles whiche cryft dyd afore his paffyon amonge whiche he fpecyallī
reherfyde the myracle that cryfte dyd in fedynge fyue thoufande people wyth
the fyue loups of brede and with iij lyttell fyfhys and thys frerys boy which
caryd not gretely for hys mafter herynge hym fay fo and confyderyng that
his mafter was fo great a churle and glotton anfwerre with a loude boyce
that all the church hard & fayd by my trouth mayfter Then there were no
frers there.whiche anfwere made all the people to fall on fuche a laughy=
nge that for fhame the frere wente out of the pulpet.and as for the frerys
boy he than departyd out of the church that the frere neuer faw hym after
By thys ye may fe that it is honefty for a mā that is at mete to depart
with fuche as he hath to them that be prefent.

Ryche fraynklyng dwellyng in the countrey had a frere vfyng to his
howfe of whom he coud neuer be ryd & had taryed with hūm the fpace
of a fenyght & neuer depart wherfore the fraynklyng beyng wery of
hym/on a tyme/as he & his wyfe & this frere fat to geder at fupper faynyd
hym felfe very angry with hys wyfe In fomoche he fayd he wolde bete her
This frere peyuyng wel what they mēt fayd thus.mafter franklig I haue
bene here this feuenyght when ye were fredys & I wyll tary here this for=
tenyght lenger but I wyll fe you frendys agayne or I go thys man perfey
uyng that he coulde no good nor wolde not depart by none honeft meanys
anfweryd hi fhortly & fayd by god frere but thou fhalte abyde here no len=
ger & toke hym by the fhulders & thruft hym out of the dorys by vyolence.

⸿ By this ye may se that he that wyll lerne no good by example / nor good maner to hym sewyd is worthy to be taught with open rebukes.

Frere Lynytour come into a pore manys howse in the countrey and because this pore man thought this frere myght do hym some good he therfore thought to make hym good chere / But bycawse hys wyfe wolde dresse hym no good mete for coste / he therfor at dyner tyme sayde thus / By god wyfe bycawse thou dyddest dresse me no good mete to my dyner / were it nat for master frere / thou sholdest haue half a dosyn stry pes Nay sir quod the frere I pray you spare nat for me / wherwith the wyf was angry & therfore at supper she cause them to fare wors.

⸿ By thys ye may se it is good polycy for gestys yf they wyll haue any good chere to pleas alway the wyfe of the howse.

Here was a frere whiche though he were well lernyd yet he was callyd wycked of condycyons whiche had a Gentylmannys sonne to wayte upon hym and to teche hym to speke latyn. ⸿ Thys frere came to thys chyldes fader dwellyng in the contrey / and because this frere wold haue this Gentylman to knowe that this chylde had merely well spent his tyme for the whyle he had bene with hym / he had this chyld to make in latyn shortly I teres walke in the cloyster. This chylde halfe astonyed bycause his master bad hym make this latyn so shortly answered at all ad uentures and sayd In circuitu impii ambulant.

In the meane tyme a good old gentylman beyng a lawyer cam to london to the terme & as he came he hapened to ouertake a frere which was som unthryft & wet alone without his beuer wherfor this gentylman asked this frere where was his beuer that shold kepe hym com pany and sayd it was contrary to his relygyon to go alone / and it wolde cause people to suppose hym to be some apostata or some unthryft. By god syr quod the frere my felow comendeth hym unto your mastershyp / who qd the gentylman I knowe hym nat / than quod the frere to the gentylman ye are the more to blame to aske for hym.

⸿ By this tale ye may se that he that geueth counsel to an unthryft and te cheth hym his dutye shall haue oftentymes but a mocke for his labour.

Here gentylmen cam into an Inne where a fayre woman was tap ster wherfor as these thre sat ther makyng mery echone of thei pray sed her I made good pastyme & plesure howbeit one spake meryly & sayd I can not se how this gentylwoman is able to make pastyme & plea sure to us all thre excepte that she were departed in thre partes. By my trouthe quod one of them / yf that she myght be so departed than I wolde chose for my parte her hed and her fayre face that I myght alway kysse her

Then quod the secōd I wold haue the brest and hart for ther lyeth her loue
Then quod the thyrd then ther is nothyng left for me but the loynys buttockys & leggys & I am content to haue yt for my part. And when these gē
tylmen had passyd the tyme ther by the space of one hour or ii they toke ther
leue & were goyng away but or thye went the thyrd man that had chosen
the bely & the buttockys dyd kys the tapyster & bad her farewel what quod
the fyrst mā that had chosen the face & the mouth why dost thou so thou dost
me wronge to kys my parte that I haue chosen of her. O quod the other I
pray the be not angry for I wolbe cōtent that thou shalt kys my part for it.

N ofter there dwellyd a mery gentylman which had a cooke callyd
Thomas that was gretly dyseasyd with the toth ake & complanyd
to his mayster therof whiche sayd he had a boke of medycis & sayd
he wold loke up his boke to se whether he cowd fynde any medecyn therfor
it & so sende one of hys doughters to his study for his boke and incontynent
lokyd uppon yt alonge season & than sayde thus to hys coke. Thomas quod
he here is a medesyne for thy tothake & yt ys a charme but it wyll do you no
good except ye knele on your knee andaske yt for seynt charyte. Thys man
glad to be relesyd of hys payne knelyd & sayd mayster for seit charyte let me
haue that medecyne. Then quod thys gentylman knele on your knees & say
after me which knelyd dose and sayd after hym as he bad hym. Thys gē
tylman began & sayd thus. The sone on the sonday The sone on the sonday
quod thomas. The mone on the monday The mone on the monday, the try
nyte on the tewiday the trinyte on the tewsday. The wite ō the wednysday
the wit on the wednysday. The holy holy thursday The holy holy thursday
And all that fast on fryday and al that fast on fryday. Shite in thy mouthe
on saterday. Thys Thomas coke heryng his mayster thus mokkyng hym
in an anger start up & sayd by goddys body mokkyng churle I wyll neuer
do the trunte more. And wente forth to hys chāber to get hys gere to geder
to thentent to gon thens by & by. But what for the anger that he toke with
hys mayster for the moke that he gaue hym & what for labour that he toke to
geder hys gere so shortly to geder the payne of the tothake wente from hym
incontynent that his mayster com to hym & made hym tary styll & tolde hym
that hys charme was the cause of the ease of the payn of his tothake.

By this tale ye may se that anger oftymes puttyth away bodely
payne.

A scoler of Orford lately made master of arte come to the cyte of lō
don & in polys met with the sayd mery gētylmā of esser which was
euer dysposyd to playe many mery patcantys with whome before
he had bene of famylier accoyntance and prayd hym to geue hym a sentence
typet This gentylman more lyberall of promys than of gyft grantyd hym
& sholde haue one yf he wolde come to his lodgynge to the signe of the bulle
without byshops gate in the nert mornynge at vi of the clocke. Thys scoler thanked hym & for that nyght departed to hys lodgynge in fletestrete/&
in the mornynge erely as he poynted cam to hym to the sygne of the bull/&
non as this gentylman saw hym he bad hym go with hym in to the Citee &
he sholde be sped anone/which incontynent went togeder tyll she cam in to
seynt laurence churche in the Jury wher the gentylman espyed a prest raue
shyd to masse & tolde the scoler that ronder is the preste that hathe the typet
for you & bade hym knele downe in the pewe & he wolde speke to hym for it/
And incontynent this gentilman went to the prest and sayd Syr here is a
scoler and kynsman of myne greatly dyseased with the chyncowgh. I pray
yow when masse ys done geue hym iij draughtys of youre chales. The prest
grauted hym & turned hym to the scoler and sayd Syr I shall serue you as
son as I haue sayd masse, the scoler the taryed styl & hard the masse trustig
then whan the masse was done that the preste wolde geue hym his typet of
sartenet. This gentylman in the meane whyle departed out of the churche
This prest whan masse was don put wyne in the chalice & cam to the scoler
knelyng in the pew profferyng hym to drink of the chales, thys scoler lokyd
vpon hym & mused & sayd/master person wherfore profer ye me the chalyce
mary quod the preste for the gentylman tolde me ye were dyseasyd with the
chicoughs prayd me therfore that for a medcyn ye myght drynk of the chalise
Nay by seynt mary quod the scoler he promysyd me ye sholdd delyuer me
a typet of sertenet. Nay sayd the preste he spake to me of no typet/but he de
syryd me to geue you drynk of the chales for the chyncough By goddys body quod the scoler he is as he was euer wont to be but a mockyng wrech/&
euer I lyue I shall quyte it hym & so departyd out of the church i greet āger

¶By thys tale ye may perceyue it were no wysdom for a man to trust to
a man to do a thynge that ys contrary to hys olde accustumyd condycyons.

It fortuned ther was a gret baryaūce betwen the byshop of Nor
which & one mayster Skelton a poyet lauriat. In somoch that the
byshope comaunded hym that he sholde nat come in at hys gatys.
This master skelton dyd absent hym selfe for a longe season but at the last
he thought to do his duty to hym and studyed wayes how he myght obtayn

the byſhopps fauour. and deterinynyd him ſelfe that he wold com to hi with
ſome preſent ⁊ humble hym ſelfe to the byſhop ⁊ gat a couple of feſants and
cam to the byſhoppys place ⁊ requyryd the porter he myght come in to ſpeke
wyth my lorde. this porter knowyng hys lordys pleaſure wolde not ſuffer
hym to come in at the gatys/wherfore this maſter ſkelton went on the bak
ſyde to ſeke ſome other way to cum in to the place. But the place was motid
that he cowd ſe no waye to come ouer except in one place where there lay a
longe tre ouer the motte in maner of a brydg that was fallyn downe with
wynd wherfore this maſter ſkelton went a long vpton the tre to com ouer
⁊ when he was almoſt ouer hys fote ſlyppid for lake of ſure fotyng ⁊ fell in
to the motte vp to the myddyl but at the laſt he recoueryd hym ſelfe ⁊ aſwel
as he coud dryed hym ſelfe agayn/⁊ ſodenly cam to the byſhop beyng in his
hall then lately ryſen from dyner which when he ſaw ſkelton comig ſo euyl
ſayd to hym why thow chatyſe I warnyd the thow ſholdys neuer come yn
at my gatys ⁊ chargyd my porter to kepe the owt. ¶ Forſoth my lorde quod
ſkelton though ye gaue ſuche charge ⁊ though your gatys be neuer ſo ſurely
kept/yet it is nomore poſſyble to kepe me owt/of your dorys, than to kepe
out crowes or pyes for I cãe not in at your gatys.but I came ou the motte
that I haue bene almoſt drownyd for my labour ⁊ ſhewd hys clothys how
euyll he was arayed which cauſyd many that ſtode thereby to laugh a pace
Then quod ſkelton yf it lyke your lordeſhyp I haue brought yow a dyſſhe
to your ſupper a coyple of Feſantys. Nay quod the byſhop I defy the and thy
Feſantys alſo And wreche as thou art pyke the out of my howſe for I wyll
none of thy gyft. How be it with as humble wordys as he coud this ſkelton
deſyryd the byſhop to be hys good lorde ⁊ to take his lytyll gyſt of hym But
the byſhop callyd hym dawe ⁊ fole often tymys ⁊ in no wyſe wolde receyue
that gyft. This Skelton than conſyderyng that the byſhop callyd hym ſole
ſo oft ſayd to one of his famylyers therby that though it were euyl to be criſ-
tynyd a ſole yet it was moche worſe to be confyrmyd a fole of ſuche a byſhop
for the name of confyrmacyõ muſt nedes a byde therfore he ymagynyd how
he might auoyd that cõfyrmaciõ ⁊ muſyd a whyl ⁊ at the laſt ſayd to the byſhop thus if your lordſhyp knew the namys of theſe feſãtys ye wold be cõtẽt
to take them/ why captyf quod the byſhop haſtely ⁊ angerly what be theyre
namys Iwys my lorde quod ſkelton this Feſant is callyd alpha.ys.primus
the fyrſt.⁊ this is callyd O that ys nouiſſimus the laſt.⁊ for the more playn
vnderſtandyng of my mide. If it pleſe your lordſhyp to take them I pmyſe
you This Alpha is the fyrſt that euer I gaue you ⁊ this O is the laſt that
euer I wyl gyue you whyl I lyue.at the which aſwer al that wer by made
gret laghter.⁊ al they deſyryd the byſhop to be good lord to hi for hys mery
conceptys at whoſe requeſt or they went the byſhop was cõtent to take hym

vnto his fauour agayn.

¶ By thys ye may se that mery conceptes dothe a man moche more good than to fret: hym selfe with anger and melancoly.

A woman of the kynges garde dwellyng in a vyllage besyde london had a very fayre yonge wyfe. To whom a carte of the towne a tal felowe resorted/& lay with her dyuers tymes whan her husband was from home/& so openly knowe that all the town spake therof/wherfor ther was a yong man of the towne well accoynted with this yeman of garde that tolde hym that suche a carter had layne by his wyfe. To whome thys yeman of garde sayd & sware by goddys body that yf he met hym it shold cost hym his lyfe. Mary quod the yong man yf ye go streyght euyn now the hye way ye shall ouertake hym dryuyng of a cart ladyn with hay toward london wherfore this yeman of garde incontynent rode after this carter/& within short space ouertoke hym & knew hym well ynough/& incontynent called the cart to hym & sayd thus Sirra I vnderstand that thou doist ly euery night with my wyfe when I am from home This carter beyng no thyng afrayd of the other/answered ye mary what than / what than quod the yeman of garde / by goddes hart haddest thou na tolde me the trouth I wolde haue broken thy hede. And so the yeman of garde retourned and no hurte done nor stroke stryken nor profered.

¶ By thys ye may se that the greatest crakers somtyme whan it cometh to the profe be moste cowardys,

In the towne of Botteley dwelled a mylner whiche had a good homely wench to his doughter whom a curat of the next towne loued/and as the same went had her at his plesure. But on a tyme this curat preched of these curyous wyues now a dayes/ & whether it were for the nones or whether it come out at all aduentures he hapned to say thus in his sermon. Ye wyues ye be so curious in all your warkes that ye wote nat what ye mene/but ye shold folowe our lady. For our lady was nothynge so curious as ye be / but she was a good homly wenche lyke the mylners doughty of botteley. At which sayng all the paryshons made gret laughynge/ & specyally they that knewe that he loued the same wenche.

¶ By this ye may se it is great foly for a man that is suspected with any parson to prayse or to name the same parson openly lest it bryng hym for ther in sclaunder.

Fole there was that dwellyd with a getylmā i the contray whiche
was callyd a great tyraunt and an extorcyoner. But this fole lo=
uyd his master metuelously because he cheryshyd hym so well.

It happenyd vppon a sea sone one of the gentylmans seruauntys
sayde to the fole, as they talkyd of sermon matters / by my trowth
Iak quod he wolde to god that thou and I were both of vs in heuyn. Nay
by lady quod the fole I wyll not go to heuyn for I had leuer go to hell than
the other askyd hym why he had leuer go to hell By my trouth quod the fole
for I wyll go with my master & I am sure my master shall go to hell / For
euery man seyth he shall go to the deuyll of hell therefore I wyll go thyther
with hym.

Here was a certayn ploughmannys sonne of the contrey of the
age ofe .xvi. yeres that neuer come moche among company but al
wey wēt to plough and husbandzy / on a tyme this yong lad wēt
to a weddynge with hys fader where he see one lute vppon a lute
And when he came home agayne at nyght his moder askyd hym
what sporte he hade at weddynge. This lad answeryd and sayd by my
trouth moder quod he ther was one that brought in a gose betwene hys ar
mys and tykled her so vppō the nek that she crekyd the swetlyest that euer
I hard gose creke in my lyfe

At a marchauntys house in london there was a mayd whiche was
gotten with chylde to whome the mastres of the house came & char=
gyd her to tell her who was the fader of the chylde. To whome the
mayden answeryd forsoth no body / why quod the maystres yt ys
not possyble but some māne muste be the fader thereof. To whome
the mayd sayd / why mastres why may not I haue a chylde without a man
as well as a hen to lay eggys wythout a cok.

Here ye may se it is harde to fynde a woman wythout
an excuse.

Gentylman there was dwellynge nygh kyngston vppon Temps.
rydynge in the contrey wyth his seruante which was not the most
quyckyst felow But rode alway sadly by hys mayster and hade ve=
ry few wordys. Hys mayster sayde to hym John quod he why ry=

dyd so sadly I wold haue the tell me som mery talys to passe the tyme with
by my trouth master quod he I can tell no talys/ why quod the master canst
not syng. no by my trouth quod hys seruaunt I coud neuer syng in all my
lyfe/ why quod the master canst thou ryme than By my trouth master quod
he I can not tell but yf ye wyll beginne to ryme I wyl solow as well as I
can by my trouth quod the master that is well layd than I wyll begyn to
make a ryme let me se howe well thou canst solowe/ so the master musyd a
whyle and than began to ryme thus. Many mennys swannes swymmyng
in temmys and so do myne. ¶ Then quod the seruaunt. And manny men
lye by other mennys wyues and so do I by thyne / what dost horson quod
the master/ by my trouth master nothynge quod he but make vp the ryme.
but quod the master I charge the tell me why thou sayst so/ forsothe master
quod he for nothynge in the worlde but to make vp your ryme. Then quod
the master yf thou do it for nothyng ellys I am content/ So the master for
gaue hym his sayinge all though he had sayd trewth.

Knyghte in Myddylsex had a seruaunt which had commytted
a felony wherof he was endyted/ and becaufe the terme drew
nye he fered he sholde be shortly arayned therof & in ieopardye
of his lyfe. wherfor in all the haste sent a letter by a walching
a seruaut of hys vnto the kynges Iustyce of the kynges bench
requyrynge hym to owe hys lawfull fauout to hys seruant and comaunded
hys seruant shortly to brynge hym an answere/ This walche man came to
the chefe Iustyce place and at the gate sawe an ape syttynge there in a cote
made for hym as they vse to apparel apys for dysport/ This walchman dyd
of hys cap & made curtesy to the ape and sayd my master recomendeth hym
to my lorde your fader & sendeth hym here a letter. Thys ape toke thys let
ter and opened it and loked theron/ and after loked vpon the man makyng
many mockes and mowes as the properte of apys is to do/ this welchman
becaufe he vnderstode hym nat came agayn to his master accordyng to his
comaundement and sayde he had delyuered the letter vnto my Lorde chefe
Iustyces sonne whiche fat at the gate in a furred cote/ And one hys master af
ked hym what answere he had whiche sayd he gaue hym an answere but it
was outher Frenche or Latyn for he vnderstode hym nat/ but syr quod he
ye nede nat to fear for I sawe by his countenance so moche that I warant
you he wyll do your errand furely to my lorde hys fader. Thys gentylman
in trust therof made none other labour. For lacke wherof hys seruant that
had done the felony within two dayes after was arayned at the kynges ben
che & cast and afterwarde hangyd.

¶ By this ye may se that euery wyse man ought to take hede that he sende no folysshe seruant vpon a hasty messa ge that is a mater of weyght.

Certayne felow there was which proffered a dagger to sell to a felowe of his whiche answered hym and sayde that he had right nought to geue hym therfor. wherfor the other sayd that he shold haue his dagger vpon condycyon that he shoulde geue and delyuer vnto hym therfore within vi. dayes after right nought / or els xl. shyllynges in money / wherto this other was content. This bargeyn thus agreyd he that sholde delyuer thys right nought toke no thought vn¬ tyll suche tyme that the day apoynted drewe nye. At the whiche tyme he be gan to Imnagyne how he myght geue hym right nought. And fyrst of all he thought on a feder / a strawe / a pynnes poynte / and suche other. But no thynge coud he deuyse but that it was somwhat / wherfore he come home al sad ꝫ pensyfe for sorow of lesynge of his xl. shyllynges / ꝫ coud nouther slepe nor take rest / wherof his wyfe beynge agreuyd demaunded the cawse of his heuynes / whiche at the last after many denayes tolde her all. well syr quod she let me herewith alone ꝫ gete ye furthe a towne / and I shall handle this well ynough. This man folowynge his wyues councell went forthe of the towne ꝫ let his wyfe shyft. ¶ This woman than henge vp an erthen pot wherof the botom was out vpon the wall by a corde. And whan this other man come ꝫ asked for the good man she sayd that he was nat within / But Syr quod she I knowe your erand wel ynough / for I wote well ye wold haue of myn husbonde xl. shyllynges because he can nat delyuer to you this day right nought / Therfore syr quod she put your hande into yonder potte and take your money / this man beyng glad thrust hir hande in supposyng to haue taken xl. shyllynges of money ꝫ thrust his hand vp through vp to the elbow / quod the wyfe than Syr what haue ye there. Mary quod he Ryght nought. Syr quod she than haue ye your bargeyn ꝫ than my husbond hath contentyd you for his dagger accordynge to his promyse.

¶ By this ye may se that often tymes a womans wyt at an extempte is moche better than a mannys.

here was a certayn lymytour which went a purtygz to a certeyn
vyllage wherin dwelled a certayn ryche man of whome he neuer
coude gette the valew of an halfpeny/yet he thought he wolde go
thyder agayn to assay theym.   And as he went thyderward the
wyfe stondynge at the dore perceyuynge hym comynge a farre of
thought that he wolde come thyder and  by & by ran in & bad her chyldren
standyng at the dore that yf the frere asked for her say she was nat within
The frere saw her ron in and suspected the cause and come to the dore and
asked for the wyfe / the chyldren as they were byddyn / sayde that she was
not within/than stode he styl lokyng on the chyldren/and at the last he cal
led to hym the eldest & bad hym let hym se hys hande/and whan he had sene
his hande O Jhesu quod he what fortune for the is ordeyned/Than called
he the seconde sonne to se hys hande/ and his hande sene the frere sayde/ O
lord what a desteny is for the prepayred.Than loked he in the thyrd sones
hand/ suerly quod he thy desteny is hardest of all/ & therwith wente he his
way.The wyfe heryng these thynges sodenly ran out and called the frere
agayne/and first made hym to come in/ and after to syt downe and set before hym the best mete that she had/and whan he had well etyn & dronken
she besought hym to tell her  the destenyes of her chyldren/which at the last
after many denayes tolde her  that the fyrst sholde be a beggar.The second
n these.The third an hompeyd/ whiche she heryng fell downe in a sowne &
toke it greuously.The frere conforted her and sayd/ that though these were
theyr fortune yet there myghte be remedy had . Than she besought hym of
his counsell.  Than sayd the frere ye must make the eldest that shalbe a beg
ger a frere.and the second that shalbe a thefe a man of law/& the thicd that
shalbe an hompeyde/a physycyon..

By this ye may lerne that they that wyll come to
the speche or presence of any parson for theyr  owne
cause they must fyrst endeuer theyr selfe to shewe
suche matters as those parsons moste delyte in.

Certeyn frere had a boy that euer was wont to bere this
freres money  and on a tyme whan the boy was farre behynde his master as they two walked togeder by the way
there met a man the frere whiche knewe that the boy bare
the freres money and sayde.  How Mayster frere / shall
I byd thy boy hye hym apace after the/ ye quod the frere

Than went ý man to ý boy ⁊ sayd spýre thy mayster bydoeth ý gyueth me
cl.d. J wyll not quod the boy then called the man with an hye boyce to ý
frere ⁊ sayd sýr he sayth he wyl not/then quod the frere be te hym/⁊ when
the boy herde his mayster say so he gaue the man.rl.pens.

By this ye maye se it is foly for a man to say ye or nay to a matter
except he knowe suerly what the matter is.

Certayn bocher dwellyng in saynt Nicholas fleshammels in lon
don callyd Poule had a seruaút callyd Peter. This Peter on a
sonday was at ý chirche heryng masse ⁊ one of his felawes who
se name was Phylip spencer was sent to call hym at the comaundement
of his mayster. So it happened at the tyme that the curat prechyd. Jnd in
his sermon touched many auctorytees of the holy scrypture. Amonge all
the wordes of the pystell of saynt Poule ad philippenses, that we be not
onely bounde to beleue in cryst but also to suffer for cryst sake ⁊ sayd the
se wordes in ý pulpet/what sayth Poule ad philippenses to this. This yõ
ge man ý was called Philip spencher had went he had spoken of hym an
swered shortely ⁊ sayd/mary sýr he bad Peter come home ⁊ take his parte
of a podyng for he sholde go for a calfe anone. The curat heryng this was
abashyd ⁊ all the audyence made grete laughter.

By this tale ye may lerne that it is no token of a wyse man to gy
ue a sodayne answere to a questyõ before that he knowe suerly what
the matter is.

Here came a courtyer by a carter the whiche in derysyon prepsed
the carters bak legges and other members of his body meruelously
whose gestyng the carter perceyued ⁊ sayd he had another properte than ý
courtyer espyed in hym/⁊ whan the courtyer had demaunded what it shol
de be/he loked a syde ouer his sholder vpon the courtyer ⁊ sayd thus/lo syr
this is my properte. J haue a wall eye in my hed/for J neuer loke ouer
my sholder this wyse but J lyghtly espye a knaue.

By this tale a man maye se that he that vsed to deryde and mocke
other folkys/is somtyme hym selfe more derpded ⁊ mocked.

A yong mã of ý age of.rr.yere rude ⁊ vnlernyd in ý tyme of lẽt cã
to his curat to be cõfessyd whiche whẽ he was of his lyfe serched
⁊ erampned coude not say his Pater noster/wherfore his cõfes

foure crossed hym to lerne his Pater noster/& shewed hym what an holy &
goodly prayer it was/& the effect therof/& the .vii. petycyons therin cōtey
ned. The fyrst petycyon begynneth. Pater noster. &c. ӱ is to saye. O fader
halowyd be thy name amōge mē in erth as amōge augels in heuen. The
ii. Ioueniat. &c. Let thy kyngdome come & regne thou amonge vs men in
erth as amonge augels in heuen. The .iii. Fiat. &c. Make vs to fulfyl thy
wyll here in erth as thy augels in heuen. The .iiii. Pane nostrū. &c. Gyue
vs our dayly sustenaūce alway & helpe vs as we gyue & helpe them ӱ haue
nede of vs. The. v. Dimitte. &c. Forgyue vs our synnes done to the as we
forgyue them ӱ trespas agaynste vs. The. vi. Et ne nos. Let vs not be
ouercome with euyll temptacyō. The .vii. Sed libera. &c. But delyuer vs
frō all euyll amen. ¶ And then his confessour after this exposycyō to hym
made inioyned hym in penaūce to fast euery fryday brede & water tyll he
had his Pater noster well & suffycyētly lerned. This yonge man mekely
acceptyng his penaūce so departed & came home to one of his cōpanyons
& sayd to his felow. so it is that my gostly fader hath gyuen me in penaūce
to fast euery fryday brede & water tyll I can say my Pater noster/therfo
re I pray ӱ teche me my Pater noster/& by my trouth I shall therfore te
che the a songe of Robyn hode that shall be worth .xx. of it.

<br>

¶ By this tale ye maye lerne to knowe the effect of the holy prayer of the
Pater noster.

<br>

A Certayn frere there was whiche vpō our lady day the Annūcy
acyon made a sermon in the whyte freyrs in London/and began
his anteteme this wyse/Aue maria gracia plena dominus tecū/
&c. ¶ These wordes quod the frere were spoken by the aungel Gabryel to
our lady when she cōceyued Cryst/whiche is as moche to say in our moder
tōgue as all heyle Mary well thou be ӱ sone of god is wt the. And further
more the augell sayd/thou shalt conceyue and bere a sone. And thou shalt
call his name Iesum/ and Elyzabeth thy swete cosyn/she shall conceyue
the swete saynt Iohn. And so procedyd styll in his Sermon in suche fonde
tyme that dyuers & many gentylmen of the court that were there begā to
smyle & laugh. The frere ӱ perceyuynge sayd thus Maysters I pray you
harke I shall tel you a narracyō. ¶ There was ones a yong preest ӱ was
not all ӱ best clark sayd masse & rede a colect thus. Deus ӱ viginti filij tui
&c. Where he sholde haue sayd vnigeniti filij tui. &c. ¶ And after whē mas
was done there was suche a gentylmā as one of you at now ӱ had herde

his maſſe came to ẏ pꝛeeſt ⁊ ſayd thus. Syꝛ I pꝛay you tell me how many
ſonnys had god almyghty/quod ẏ pꝛeeſt why aſke you ẏ. Mary ſyꝛ quod ẏ
gentylman I ſuppoſe he had.xx. ſonnys/foꝛ ye ſayd ryght now. Deus qui
biginti filii tui. The pꝛeeſt perceyuyng how ẏ he derydyd hym anſwerde
hym ſhoꝛtly ⁊ ſayd thus. How many ſonnys ſo euer god almyghty had/
I am ſure ẏ thou art none of them foꝛ ẏ ſkoꝛnyſt ẏ woꝛde of god. And ſoo
ſayd the frere in the pulpet. No moꝛe at ye none of ẏ chylderē of god. Foꝛ
ye ſkoꝛne ⁊ laugh/at me now ẏ pꝛeche to you the woꝛde of god. whych woꝛ
dys made the gentylmen and all the other people laughe moche moꝛe thā
they dyd befoꝛe.

¶ By this tale a man may lerne to perceyue well ẏ the beſt the wyſyſt
⁊ ẏ moſt holpeſt matter ẏ is by found pꝛonunciacyon ⁊ vtteraūce may
be marryd/noꝛ ſhall noꝛ edyfye to ẏ audyēce. Therfoꝛe euery pꝛoces
wolde be vtteryd with woꝛdys ⁊ cōtenaūce conuenyent to the matter.
¶ Alſo yet by this tale they that be vnlernyd in ẏ latyn tongue maye
knowe the ſentence of the aue maria.

I¶ Na vyllage in warwyck ſhere there was a paryſhe pꝛeeſt ⁊ thoughe he were no gret clark noꝛ graduat of ẏ vnyuerſytye/yet he pꝛe
chyd to his paryſhons vpō a ſonday/declaryng to thē ẏ. xii. atty-
cles of the Crede. ſhewynge them that the fyꝛſt attycle was to beleue in
god the fader almyghty maker of heuen ⁊ erth. The ſecond. To beleue in
Ieſu Cryſte his onely ſone our loꝛde coequall with ẏ fader in all thynges
perteynyng to ẏ deyte. The thyꝛd that he was cōceyuyd of the holy gooſt
Boꝛne of the vyꝛgyn Mary. The fourth that he ſuffred deth vnder ponce
pylate/⁊ that he was crucyfyed dede ⁊ beryed. The fyſt that he deſcendyd
to hel ⁊ fet out ẏ good ſowlys ẏ were in fayth ⁊ hope/and that he ẏ thyꝛd
day roſe from deth to lyfe. The ſyrth he aſſendyd in to heuen to ẏ ryght ſyde of god ẏ fader wher he ſyttyth. The ſeuenth ẏ he ſhall come at the day
of dome to Iudge both vs that be quyk ⁊ them that be dede. The eyght to
beleue in the holy gooſt equall god w̄ the fader ⁊ the ſone . The nynth in
holy chyꝛche Catholyke ⁊ in ẏ holy comunyō of ſayntys. The tenth In ẏ
remyſſyon of ſynnes. The leuynth In the reſurreccyō generall of ẏ body
⁊ ſoule. The twelfth In euerlaſtynge lyfe that god ſhall reward thē that
be good. And ſayd to his paryſhons further ẏ theſe artyclesye be boūde
to beleue foꝛ they be trewe ⁊ of auctoꝛyte. And yf you beleue not me/thē loꝛ
a moꝛe ſuerte ⁊ luffycyēt auctoꝛyte/go your way to couentre/and there ye

ye ſhall ſe them all playd in coꝛpus criſti playe.

⸿ By redyng of this tale they ꝑ vnderſtode no latyn may lerne to kno
we the .xii. articles of the fayth.

ALimitour of the gray frerys in London whiche pꝛechyd in a cer
tayn vyllage in the countrey in the tyme of his lymitacyõ / ⁊ had
but one ſermõ which he had lerned by hart ꝑ was of ꝑ declaryng
of the .x. cõmaũdementes. The fyꝛſt to beleue in one god / ⁊ to honour hym
aboue all thynge. The ſecõd to ſwere not in vayn by hym noꝛ none other
of his creatures. The thyꝛde to abſteyne from woꝛdly operacyõ on ꝑ holy
day thou ⁊ all thy ſeruantys of whõ thou haſt charge. The fourthe to ho
noꝛ thy parẽtys ⁊ helpe thẽ in theyꝛ neceſſyte. The fyfth to ſle no man in
dede noꝛ wyll noꝛ foꝛ no hated hurte his body noꝛ good name. The ſyxt te
do no foꝛnycacyõ actuall / noꝛ by no vnlefull thought to deſyꝛe no fleſhly
delectacyõ. The ſeuenth to ſtele noꝛ depꝛyue no mãnes goodes by thefte
robbery extoꝛcyõ / vſery / noꝛ dyſceyt. The eyght to bere no falſe wytneſſe
to hurt another / noꝛ to tell no lyes / noꝛ to ſay nothyng agaynſt trewthe.
The nynth to couet noꝛ deſyꝛe no mãnys goodys vnlefull. The tenth to
couet noꝛ to deſyꝛe thy neyghbours wyfe foꝛ thyn owne appetyte vnleful
ly. ⸿ And becauſe this frere had pꝛeched this ſermon ſo oftyn / one ꝑ had
hard it befoꝛe told the frerys ſeruaũt ꝑ his mayſter was callyd frere Johñ
x. cõmaũdementes wherfoꝛ this ſeruaũt ſhewed ꝑ frere his mayſter ther
of / and aduyſed hym to pꝛeche ſome ſermon of ſome other matter / foꝛ it
greuyd hym to here his mayſter ſo deryded / ⁊ to be called frere Johñ .x. cõ
maũdemẽtys / foꝛ euery man knoweth what ye wyll ſay as ſoone as euer
ye begyn bycauſe ye haue pꝛeched it ſooft. ⸿ Why than quod ꝑ frere I am
ſure thou knoweſt well whiche be ꝑ x. cõmaũdementys ꝑ haſt harde thẽ ſo
oft declaryd / ye ſyꝛ quod the ſeruaũt ꝑ I do. Then quod the frere I pꝛaye
the reherſe thẽ vnto me now. Mary quod ꝑ ſeruaũt theſe be they. Pꝛyde
Couetyſe Slouth Enuy wꝛath Glotony and Lechery.

⸿ By redynge this tale ye maye lerne to knowe the .x. cõmaundeme
tes and the .vii. dedely ſynnes.

THe huſbande ſayde to his wyfe thus / wyfe by this candell I dre
med this nyght that I was a cokcolde. To whome ſhe anſwered
and ſayd huſbonde. By this bꝛede ye are none. Thẽ ſayd he / wyfe ete the

bꝛede. She anſwerd & ſayd to her huſbande/then ete you the candell foꝛ you ſware fyꝛſt.

¶ By this a man may ſe that a womans anſwere is neuer to ſeke.

A woman demaūdyd a queſtyon of a yong chyld ſonne vnto a mā of lawe of what craft his fader was/which chyld ſayd his fader was a crafty man of lawe.

¶ By this tale a man may perceyue that ſome tyme peraduenture yōg innocentys ſpeke truely vnaduyſed.

IN a certayn paryſh chyꝛche in London after the olde lawdable & accuſtomyd maner there was a frere mynoꝛ all thoughe he were not the beſt clarck noꝛ coude not make the beſt ſermon/ yet by the lycence of the curat he there pꝛeched to the paryſhous. Among the whiche audyence there was a wyfe at that tyme lytyll dyſpoſyd to contemplacyō talkyd with a goſyp of hers of other femynyne tales/ſo loud that the frere hard & ſomwhat was perturbyd therwith. To whom therfoꝛe openly the frere ſpake & ſayd. Thou woman there in the tawny gown/hold thy peace & leue thy babelyng thou troblyſt the woꝛde of god. ¶ This woman there with ſodeynly abaſſhyd bycauſe ɏ frere ſpake to her ſo openly ɏ al ɏ people her beheld anſweryd ſhoꝛtly & ſayd/ I beſhꝛewe her hard that babelyd mo re of vs two. At ɏ whyche ſeyng ɏ people dyd laugh bycauſe they felt but lytyll fruyte in his ſermon.

¶ By this tale a man may lerne to be ware how he openly rebukyth a ny other & in what audyence leſt it tourne to his owne repꝛofe.

IN the rayne of the moſt myghty and vyctoꝛyous Pꝛynce kynge Henry the.viii. cruell warre began betwene Engliſhe men & Fren ſhemen/& Skottys. The Engliſhemen were ſo myghty vpon ɏ ſe that none other people of other realmys were able to reſyſt thē/ wherfo re they toke many greꝛ enterpꝛyſys/& many ſhyppys/& many pꝛyſoners of other remys ɏ were theꝛ enmys. Among the which they happenyd on a ſeaſon to take a ſkottys ſhyp.& dyuers ſkottys they ſlew & toke pꝛyſoners Among whom ther was a welchmā that had one of the ſkottys pꝛyſoner & bad hym that he ſhold do of his harnes/which to do the Skot was very loth/howbeyt foꝛ fere at ɏ laſt he pullyd it of w an yuyll wyll/ & ſayde to

D.iii.

ꝑ welchmā/yf thou wilt nedys haue my.harnes take it there/⁊ caſt it ouer
the boꝛd in to the ſe.The welchman ſeyng that ſayd.By Cottes blut ⁊ her
nayll. J ſhal make her fat it agayn.And toke hym by ꝑ legges ⁊ caſt hym
after ouer the boꝛd in to the ſe.

¶By this tale a man maye lerne ꝑ he that is ſubget to another ought
to foꝛſake his owne wyll/⁊ folow his wyll ⁊ cōmaūdement ꝑ ſo hath
ſubiectyon ouer hym/leſt it toꝛne to his gretter hurt ⁊ damage.

Here was a man that maryed a woman whiche hath grete ryches
⁊ bewte/how be it ſhe had ſuche an impedyment of nature that ſhe
was domeand coude not ſpeke/whiche thynge made hym full ofte to be
ryght penſyfre ⁊ ſad/wherfoꝛe vpon a daye as he walkyd alone ryght heuy
in hart thynkig vpō his wyfe.There came one to hym ⁊ aſkyd hym what
was the cauſe of his heuynes/which anſweryd that is was onely bycauſe
his wyfe was boꝛne dome.To whō this other ſayd.J ſhall ſhewe ꝑ ſoone
a remedy ⁊ a medycyn therfoꝛe that is thus.Go take an aſpenleſe ⁊ lap it
vnder her tōgue this nyght ſhe beyng a ſlepe/ ⁊ J warrant the ꝑ ſhe ſhall
ſpeke on the moꝛow/whiche man beyng glad of this medycyne pꝛeparyd
therfoꝛe/⁊ gatheryd aſpen leues.Wherfoꝛe he layd.iii.of them vnder her
tōge whē ſhe was aſlepe.And vpon ꝑ moꝛowe whē he hym ſelf wakyd he
deſpꝛous to know how his medycyne wꝛoughte beyng in bed w her he de
maunded of her how ſhe dyd/⁊ ſodenly ſhe anſweryd ⁊ ſayd. J beſhꝛewe
your hart foꝛ wakynge me ſo erly/ ⁊ ſo by bertew of ꝑ medycyne ſhe was
reſtoꝛed to her ſpeche.¶But in cōcluſyon her ſpeche ſo increſyd day by day
⁊ ſhe was ſo curſt of cōdycyō that euery day ſhe bꝛaulyd ⁊ chyde with her
huſbande ſo moche ꝑ at ꝑ laſt he was moꝛe beryd and had moche moꝛe tro
ble ⁊ dyſſeaſe with her ſhꝛewed woꝛdes then he had befoꝛe whan ſhe was
dome.¶Wherfoꝛe as he walked another tyme alone he happened to mete
agayne with the ſame perſon that taught hym the ſayde medycyne. And
ſayde to hym this wyſe¶Syꝛ ye taught me a medycyne but late to make
my dome wyfe to ſpeke.By doyng me laye an aſpen leſe vnder her tonge
when ſhe ſlepte.And J layd.iii.aſpen leues there. wherfoꝛe now ſhe ſpe
keth.But yet ſhe ſpeketh ſo moche and ſo ſhꝛewdly that J am moꝛe wery
of her now than J was befoꝛe when ſhe was dome.¶Wherfoꝛe J pꝛaye
you teche me a medycyne to modyfye her that ſhe ſpeke not ſo moche.
¶This other anſweryd and ſayd thus.Syꝛ J am a deuyll of hell. But J
am one of them that haue leeſt power there.Albeyt yet J haue power to
make a woman to ſpeke.But yet yf a woman begyn ones to ſpeke/ J noꝛ

all the dyuels in helle that haue the most power be not able to make a wo
man to be styll/noz to cause her to leue her spekynge.

¶ By this tale ye may note that a man oftymes despzeth and coueteth
to moche that thynge that oft tozneth to his dysplesure.

One askyd a proctoure of the Arches lately befoze maryed why he
chase hym so lytell a wyfe/whiche answerde because he had a text
saynge thus. Et duobus malis minus malum est eliendum./that is
to saye in englysshe. Amonge euyll thynges the lest is to be chosen.

IN the tyme of lente there cam two nonnys to saynt Johns in lon
don bycause of the greate pardon there to be confessyd. Of ý whiche nonnys the one was a yonge lady & the other was olde. This
yonge lady chose fyzst her Confessoure/and confessyd her that she had synned in Lechery. The confessoure asked w̃ whom it was. She sayde it was
with a lusty Gallãt. He demaũdyd where it was. She sayd in a pleasaunt
grene herber. He askyd further whẽ it was. She sayd in ý mery moneth of
May. Then sayd ý confessour this wyse. I fayze yonge lady/with a lusty
gallant/in a pleasaunt herber/in ý mery moneth of May/ye dyd but pour
kynde. Now by my trouth god fozgyue you & I do. ¶ And so she departed
and incõtynent the olde nõne met with her askynge her how she lyked her
confessour/whiche sayde that he was the best gostly fader ý euer she hadde
and the most easyst in penaunce geuynge. ¶ Foz cõfozt wherof this other
nonne went to the same confessour. And shzoue her lyke wyse that she had
synned in Lechery. And he demaunded with whom/which sayde with an
olde Frere/he askyd where. She sayd in her olde cloyster. He askyd what
season. She sayd in lent. Then the confessour sayd thus. ¶ In olde hoze to
lye with an olde frere/in the olde cloyster/in the holy tyme of Lent. By
cokkys body yf god fozgyue the yet wyll I neuer fozgyue the. ¶ Whiche
wozdys causyd her to departe all sad and soze abasshyd.

¶ By this tale men may lerne that a vycyouse acte is moze abhomyna
ble in one person than in an other/in one season than in an other and
in one place than in an other.

Hen the most noble and fortunate pzynce kynge Edwarde of Englonde made warre in Fraunce with a greatte puysshaunce and
Armye of People. ¶ Whome the Frenche kynge with a nother

grete hoſt incounterpd. And whan bothe ꝑ hoſtis ſhulde Joyne ⁊ the trum
pettis began to blow/a yong ſquyer of englonde rydyng on a luſty courſer
of whiche horſe the noyſe of ꝑ trupettys ſo prykkyd ꝑ courage ꝑ the ſquyer
coude not hym retayne/ſo that agaynſt his wyll he ran vpon his enemys
whiche ſquyer ſeynge none other remedy ſet his ſpere in the reſt/and rode
through the thykkyſt of his enemys/⁊ inconcluſyon had good fortune and
ſaurd hymſelfe alyue without hurt/⁊ the englyſh hoſt folowed ⁊ had the
vyctory. And after when ꝑ felde was done this kyng Edwarde called the
ſquyer/⁊ bad hym knele downe for he wolde make hym knyght/becauſe ꝑ
he valyauntly was ꝑ men ꝑ day which with the moſt couragyouſe ſtomak
aduenturyd fyrſt vpon theyr enemys. To whom ꝑ ſquyre this anſwerde:
yf it lyke your grace to make any body knyght therfore/I beſeche you to
make my horſe knyght ⁊ not me/for certes it was his dede ⁊ not myne/⁊
full ſore agaynſt my wyll. ⁋Whiche anſwere the kynge herynge reſtray
nyd to promote hym to the order of knyghthode/reputynge hym in maner
but a cowarde/⁊ euer after fauoryd hym the leſſe.

⁋By this tale a man may lerne how it is wyſdome for one that is in
good credence to kepe hym therin/and in nowyſe to dyſable hymſelfe
to mocht.


A yonge man late maryed to a wyfe thought it was good polycy,
to get the mayſtry of her in the begynnynge. Cam to her the pot
ſethyſige ouer ꝑ fyre all though the mete therin were not inough
ſodenly comaundyd her to take the pot from the fyre. whyche anſweryd ⁊
ſayde that ꝑ mete was not redy to ete. And he ſayd agayne I wyll haue it
taken of for my pleaſure. This good woman loth yet to offend hym ſet ꝑ
pot beſyde the fyre/as he had. And anone after he comaunded her to ſet the
pot behynde the dore/⁊ ſhe ſayd therto agayne ye be not wyſe therin. But
he preciſely ſayd it ſholde be ſo as he bad. And ſhe gentyly agayne dyd his
comaundement. This man yet not ſatyſfyed comaunded her to ſet the pot a
hygh vpon the hen roſt/what quod ꝑ wyf agayne I trow ye be mad. And
he fyerſly than comaunded her to ſet it there or els he ſayd ſhe ſholde repet
She ſomewhat aferde to mone his pacience toke a ladder and ſet it to the
rooſt/and wet herſelf vp the ladder and toke the pot in her hande prayeng
her huſbande than to holde the ladder faſt for ſlydynge whiche ſo dyd.
⁋And whenne the huſbande lokyd vp and ſawe the potie ſtande there
an hyght he ſayd thus. Lo now ſtandyth the pot there as I wolde haue it

This wyfe herynge that sodenly pouryd the hote potage on his hed & sayd thus. And now bene the potage there as I wolde haue them.

By this tale men may se it is no wysedome for a man to attempte a meke womãs pacyence to far lest it torne to his owne hurte & damynage

A Certayne confessour in the holy tyme of lente inioyned his penitent to say dayly for his penaunce this prayer. Agnus dei mise rere mei/whiche was as moche to saye in englyshe as ye Lambe of god haue mercy vpon me. This penitens acceptynge his penaunce depar tyd & that tyme twelfe moneth after came agayne to be confessyd of the same côfessoure whiche demaundyd of hym whether he had fulfyllyd his penaunce that he hym inioynyd ye last yere. And he sayd thus/ye syr I thank god I haue fulfylled it / for I haue sayde thus to daye mornynge and so dayly. The shepe of god haue mercy vpon me. To whom the confessour sayd. Nay I bad ye say a gnus dei miserere mei/that is ye lambe of god haue mercy vpon me. ye syr quod ye penytent ye say trouth that was ye laste yere/but now it is at twelfe month syth/& it is a shepe by this tyme. Therfore I must nedys say now ye shepe of god haue mercy vpon me.

By this tale ye may perceyue that yf holy scrypture be expownyd to rude Lay people onely in the lytterall scence. Peraduenture it shal do but lytell good.

IT fortuned dyuers to be in comunycacyon amonge whom there was a curat or a paryssh preest & one John daw a parysshon of his whiche .ii. had comunycacyon more busy than other in this maner This preest thought ye one myght not by felynge knowe one from another in the darke/ John daw his parysshon of contrary oppynyon layde with his curate for a wager .xi. pence. Wherupon the paryssh preest wyllynge to proue his wager wente to this John dawes house in the euenynge and sodenly gate hym to bed with his wyfe where whē he began to be somwhat besy. She felynge his crowne sayde shortly with a loude voyce. By god thou art not John daw. That herynge her husbond answerde. Thou lyst trouth wyfe I am here John daw. Therfore mayster person gyue me the money for ye haue lost your .xi. pence.

By this tale ye may lerne to perceyue yt it is no wysedome for a man for ye couetouse of wynnyng of any wager to put in Ieopardy a thyng that may come hym to gretter dyſplaſure.

¶A Rych frankelyn in ẏ contrey hauynge by his wyfe but one chyld
and no mo for the grete affeccyon that he had to his ſayde chylde
founde hym at Oxford to ſcole by the ſpace of .ii.or.iii.yere. This
yonge ſcoller in a bocacyon tyme for his diſport came home to his fader.
¶It fortuned afterwarde in a nyght the fader ẏ moder & the ſayde yonge
ſcoller ſyttynge at ſupper hauynge before them no more mete but onely a
cople of chykyns the fader ſayd this wyfe. Sone ſo it is that I haue ſpent
moch money vpon the to fynde ẏ to ſcole / wherfore I haue grete deſyre to
know what haſt lernyd. To whom ẏ ſone anſwerde & ſayde. Fader I haue
ſtudyed ſoueſtrye & by that ſcyence I can proue ẏ theſe.ii.chykyns in ẏ dyſſh
be thre chykyns. Mary ſayd ẏ fader that wolde I fayne ſe. The ſcoller toke one of ẏ chykyns in his hand & ſayd. Lo here is one chykyn / and incõtynent he toke both ẏ chykyns in his hand ioyntly & ſayd here is .ii. chykyns
and one &.ii.maketh.iii. Ergo here is.iii.chykyns. Then ẏ fader toke one
of the chykyns to hymſelfe and gaue another to his wyfe & ſayd thus. Lo
I wyll haue one of ẏ chykyns to my parte / & thy moder ſhall haue another
& bycauſe of thy good argument thou ſhalt haue ẏ thyrde to thy ſupper / for
thou getteyſt no more mete here at this tyme / whiche promyſe the fader
kept & ſo the ſcoller went without his ſupper.

¶By this tale men may ſe that it is grete foly to put one to ſcole to lerne any ſubtyll ſcyence whiche hath no naturall wytte

¶A Frere of london there was that on a ſondaye mornynge early in
ẏ ſomer ſeaſõ came from Londõ to Barnet to make a colacyon /
& was there an houre before hye maſſe began / & bycauſe he wolde
come to ẏ chyrch honeſtly / he went fyrſt to an alehouſe there to wype his
ſhops & to make hymſelf clenely. In the whiche houſe there were podyngis
to ſelle / & dyuers folkys there brekynge theyr faſt & etyng podyngys. But
ẏ frere brake his faſt in a ſecrete place & in ẏ ſame hous. ¶This frere ſoone
after came to the chyrch and by lycence of ẏ curat enteryd in to the pulpet
to make a colacyon or ſermon. And in his ſermon there he rebukyd ſore ẏ
maner of them that vſyd to broke theyr faſt on the ſondaybefore hye maſſe
& ſayd it was called ẏ dpuyls blak brekfaſt. And with that worde ſpekyng
as he dyd caſt his armys out to make his coũtenaũce there fell a podynge
out of his ſleue / whiche he hymſelf had ſtolẽ a lytel before in ẏ ſame alehous

¶When ꝑ people ſawe that ⁊ ſpecyally they ꝑ brake theyꝛ faſt there ꝑ ſame moꝛnyng ⁊ anew wel that ꝑ wyfe had compleyned how ſhe had one of her podynges ſtolyn/they laughyd ſo moche at the frere ꝑ he incontynent went downe of the pulpet foꝛ ſhame.

¶By this tale a man may ſe that whē a preacher doth rebuke any ſynne oꝛ vyce wherin he is knowē openly to be gylty hymſelf/ſuche preachyng ſhall lytell edyfy to the people.

A Certayne ſkoller ther was intendynge to be made preſt whiche had nother grete wytte noꝛ lernyng came to the byſſhop to take oꝛders/whos folyſſhneſſe ꝑ byſſhop perceyuyng becauſe he was a ryche mānes ſon wolde not very ſtrongly appoſe hym but aſkyd hym this ſmall queſtyon. Noe had.iiij.ſonnes/ Sem/Cham ⁊ Japhet/now tell me quod ꝑ byſſhop wo was Japhetis father ⁊ thou ſhalt haue oꝛders. Then ſayd ꝑ ſcoler By my trouth my loꝛde I pray you pardō me. Foꝛ I neuer ler nyd but lytell of the byble. Then quod the byſſhop/go home ⁊ come agayn ⁊ ſoyle me this queſtyon ⁊ thou ſhalt haue oꝛders. ¶This ſcoler ſo depar ted ⁊ came home to his fader ⁊ ſhewde hym ꝑ cauſe of the hynderaunce of his oꝛders. ¶His fader beynge angry at his folyſſhnes thought to teche hym ꝑ ſolucyon of this queſtyon by a famplyer example ⁊ called his ſpany els befoꝛe hym ⁊ ſayd thus/thou knowyſt well Coll my dogge hath theſe iij. whelpys Ryg/Tryg/⁊ Tryboll Muſt not Coll my dog nedys be Syre to tryboll. Then quod the ſcoler by god fader ye ſaye trouth let me alone now/ye ſhall ſe me do well ynough ꝑ nexte tyme. wherfoꝛe on ꝑ moꝛowe he wente to ꝑ byſſhop agayne ⁊ ſayd he coud ſoyle his queſtyon. Then ſayd the byſſhop Noe had. iij. ſonnes Sem Cham ⁊ Japhet/now tell me who was Japhetys fader Mary ſyꝛ quod ꝑ ſcoler yf it pleaſe your loꝛdſhyp Col my faders dog.

¶By this tale a man may lerne that it is but loſt tyme to teche a fole any thynge whych hath no wyt to perceyue it.

I T foꝛtuned ſo that a frere late in the euenynge deſyꝛed lodgynge of a pooꝛe man of the countrey/the whiche foꝛ lake of other lod gynge glad to herboꝛowe the frere lodgyd hym in his owne bed. And after he and his wyfe. The frere beynge a ſleepe came and lay in the ſame bedde. ¶And in the moꝛnynge after the pooꝛe man ro ſe and wente to the marketh leuynge the Frere in ꝑ bedde with his wyfe

And as he went he smyled & laughyd to hymselfe / wherfore his neybours demaunded of hym why he so smyled / he answerd & sayd I laugh to thynk how shamefast the frere shall be when he waketh / whom I left in bedde with my wyfe.

¶ By this tale a man may lerne that he that ouershotyth hymself doth folyshly yet he is more fole to shewe it openly.

Sometyme there dwellyd a preist in Stretforth vpon a vyce of small lernynge whiche vndeuoutly sange masse / & often tymes twyse on one day. So it happened on a tyme after his seconde mas was done in shote rey not a myle from Stretforth there mete with hym dyuers merchaunt men whiche wolde haue harde masse / & desyred hym to synge masse and he sholde haue a grote / whiche answerd them & sayd Syrs I wyll say masse no more this day / but I wyl say you .ii. gospels for one grote / & that is dog chepe a masse in ony place in englonde.

¶ By this tale a man may se that they that be rude & vnlernyd regard but lytell the meryt & goodnes of holy prayer.

A Courtyer & a frere happenyd to mete togyder in a fery bote & in comunycacyon betwene them fell at wordys angry & dyspleasyd eche with other / & fought & strogled togyder / so that at the last the courtyer cast the frere ouer the bote / so was the frere drowned. The feryman whiche had ben a man of warre the most parte of his lyfe before and seynge the frere was so drowned & gon sayde this to the courtyer / I beshrewe thy hart thou sholdest haue taryed & foughte with hym a lande for nowe thou hast caused me to lese an halfpeny for my fare.

¶ By this tale a man may se that he that is accostumed in vycyous & cruel company shall lose that noble bertew to haue pyte & compassyon vpon his neyghboure.

A Precher in the pulpet whiche prechyd the worde of god / & among other matters spake of mennys soullys & sayd they were so meruelous & so subtyll that a thousand soullys myght daunce in the space of a naple of a mannys fynger / amonge whiche audyence there was a mery conceyted felowe of smal deuocyon that answerde and sayd this / mayster doctor yf that a thousande soullys may daunce on a mannys nayle I pray you tell then where shall the pyper stande.

¶ By this tale a man may se that it is but foly to shewe or to teche bertew to them that haue no pleasure nor mynde therto.

In londo there was a certayn artyfycer hauyng a fayre wyf to who a lusty galat made pursute to accomplyshe his pleasur. This woma

denyenge sholde the matter vnto her husbande /whiche moupd therwith
had his wyfe to appoynte hym a tyme to come secretly to lye with her all
nyght. And w gret krakys & othes sware y agaynst his lyf except coming
he wolde be redy harnesyd & wolde put hym in ieopcrdy of his comyng he
wolde make hym a grete amendys. This nyght was them appoynted at
whiche tyme this courtyer came at his howre & entred into the chaumber
set his two handswozde downe & sayde these wozdes. Stand thou there
thou swozde the deth of .iii. men. This husbande lyenge vnder y bed in
harnes heryng these wozdes lay styl foz fere. The courtyer anone gat hym
to bed with the wyfe aboute his pzepensyd besynes / and within an houre
oz.ii. the husbande beynge wery of lyenge began to remoue hym /the cour
tyar that herynge askyd the wyfe what thynge that was y remouyd vnder y bed /whiche exculyng y matter sayde it was a lytell shepe that was
wonte dayly to go about the hous & the husbande y herynge anone cryed
ble as it had ben a shepe. And so inconclusyon when y courtyer saw his ty
me he rose & kyssed the wyfe & toke his leue & departyd. And as soone as he
was gone the husbande arose /& when the wyfe lokyd on hym somwhat a-
bashyd she began to make a sad coutenaunce & sayde Alas syz why dyd ye
not ryse & play the man as ye sayde ye wolde /whiche answerde and sayde
why dame dydest thou not here hym say that his swozde had ben the dethe
of .iii. men / & I had bena fole than yf y I had put my selfe in ieopardy to
haue ben the fourth. Then sayd the wyfe thus /but syz spake not I wysely
then when I sayd ye were a shepe /yes quod y husbande. But than dyd not
I moze wysely dame when that I cryed ble.

By this ye maye se that he is not wyse that wyll put his confy-
dens to moche vpon these grete crakers whiche oftymes wyll do
but lytell when it comyth to the poynt.

There was a shomaker syttynge in his shop y sawe a colyer come by
thought to deryde hym bycause he was so blacke / askyd hym what
thydynges were in hell and how the deuyll faryed. To whome the colyer
sayde /the deuyll fared well when I sawe hym last foz he was rydynge
foz the and taryed but foz a sowter to pluk on his botis.

By this ye may se that he that vsyth to deryde other folkys is
somtyme hymselfe moze derydyd and mokkyd.

C.i.

I fynde wrytt amonge olde gestys how god made saynte peter porter of heuen/ and that god of his goodnes soone after his passyon
suffred many men to come to the kyngdome of heuen with small
deseruyng/at whiche tyme there was in heuen a grete company of wel-
chemen/whiche with thyre krakynge & babelynge trobelyd all the other.
wherfore god sayd to saynt peter ý he was wery of them/& that he wolde
fayne haue them out of heuen. To whome saynt Peter sayde good lorde I
warrant you ý shalbe shortly done wherfore saynt peter went out of he-
ue gatys & cryed w a loude voyce Cause bobe/ý is as moche to say as rostyd
chese/whiche thynge ý welchmen heryng ran out of heuen a gret pace.
And when saynt Peter sawe them al out he sodenly went in to heuen and
lokkyd the dore and so sparryd all the welchemen out.

¶ By this ye may se that it is no wysdome for a man to loue or to set his
mynde to moche vpon ony delycate or wordly pleasure wherby he shall
lose the celestyall & eternall Joye.

Two knyghtes there were whiche went to a stondyng felde w theyr
prynce. But one of them was cofessyd before he went/but the other
went in to ý felde without shryft or repetaunce/afterward this price wa ý felde
& had ý byctorye ý day/wherfore he ý was cofessyd came to ý price & askyd
an office & sayd he had deseruyd it for he had don good seruyce & aduentured
that day as far as ony man in ý felde/ to whom the other ý was vncofessyd
answeryd and sayd nay by the mas I am more worthy to haue a rewarde
than he/for he aduenturyd but his body for your sake for he durst not go to
ý felde tyl he was cofessyd/but as for me I dyd iupd both body lyfe & soule for your sake/for I went to the felde without cofessyon or repentaunce.

A Certayn mylner ther was which had dyuers poundys of elis wher
was good store of elys/wherfore ý pson of ý town whiche lokyd
like a holy man dyuers & many timis stale many of the in so moche
ý he had left few or none behind him/wherfore this milner seyng his elis
stolyn & wuit not by whom cam to ý sayd pson & desired hym to curse for the
ý pson sayd he wolde.& ý next soday ca in to ý pulpet w book bell & candell
& preuyng there were none in ý chirche ý vnderstode latyn sayd thus/he ý
stale ý milners elis laudate dum de celis but he ý stale ý grer elis grudeat
ipse in celis/ ther w put out ý candell who syr quod ý mylner no more for
this sauce is sharp ynough for hym.                    ¶ By this ye may se
that some curatys that loke full holyly be but dessemblers & ppocrytis.

A welchema on a tyme went to chirche to here mas whiche hapenyd
to come in euyn at ý sacryng time when he had hayd ý mas to ý ende
he wet home wher one of his felowes askyd hym whether he had sene god
almighty to day which a sweryd & sayd nay but I saw one rl.s. better tha he
        ¶ By this ye mare se that they be euyll brought vp haue but lytyll
deuocyon to pray and vertew.

Upon a tyme certayn women in the countrey were appoynted to de
ryde and mokke a frere a lymptour that vsyd moche to vpsyth them
wherupon one of them a lytyll before that the frere came kylled an hog &
for dyspozt seyd it vnder the borde after the maner of a corse and tolde the
frere it was her good mã and desyzed hym to say dirige for his soule wher
fore the frere and his fela w began Placebo and Dirige and so forth sayd
the seruyse full deuowtly which the wyues so heryng/coude not refrayne
them selfe from lawghynge and wente in to a lytyll parler to lawgh mo
re at theyr plesure. These frerys somwhat suspected the cause and quykly
or that y women were ware lokyd vnder the borde and spyed that it was
an hog/sodenly toke it bytwene them and bare it homeward as fast they
myght. The women seyng that ran after the frere and cryed come agayn
mayster frere come agayne and let it all one/nay by my fayth quod y frere he is a broder of oures and therfore he must nedys be buryed in oure cloy
ster/and so the frerys gate the hog.

¶By this ye may se that they that vse to deryde and mok other somtyme it tornyth to theyr one losse and damage.

A Certayne preest there was that dwellyd in y countrey which was
not very lernyd. Threfore on Eester euyn he set his boy to y preest
of the nert town y was, ii. myle from thens to know what masse
he sholde synge on y morowe. This boy came to the sayd preest and dyd his
maysters errãde to hym. Then quod the preest tel thy mayster that he must
synge to morow of the resurrexyon/and furthermore quod he yf thou hap
to forget it tel thy mayster that it begynneth w a gret R. and shewed hym
the masse booke where it was wryten Resurreri. &c. This boy than wente
home agayne and all the way as he went he clateryd styll. Resurreri Re-
surreri/but at y last he hapenyd to forget it clene and whẽ he came home
his mayster askyd hym what masse he sholde synge on y morowe. By my
troth mayster quod the boy I haue forgoten it/but he bad me tell you it be
gã w a gret. R. By god quod the preest I trowe thou sayest trewth for now
I remember well it muste be requiem eternam/for god almyghty dyed as
on yester day & now we must say masse for his soule.

¶By this ye may se that when one fole sendyth another fole on his er
rand oftentymes the besynes is folysshly spede.

A Skoler of Drenford whiche had studyed y iudycyals of astrono
my õ a tyme was rydyng by y way which cã by a herdmã & inquy
red of hym how far it was to y nert town/syz qd y herdmã ye ha
ue nott hyd past a myle & ã half /but syz qd he ye nede to ryde a pace for ye
shal haue a shour of rayner ye côe thyder/what qd y skoler y is not so for he
re is no token of rayn for all y cloudys be both fayr & clere/by god syz qd y

E.ii.

herd man but ye shall fynd it so. The skoler then rode forth his way & or he
had ryden half a myle forther there fel a good showre of rayn that the sko
ler was well wasshyd and wete to ye skyn/ ye skoler then tournyd his horse
and rode agayne to the herdman & desyred hym to teche hym that connyng
nay quod ye herdman I wyll not teche you my connynge for nought/ tha
the skoler profferyd hym .xl. shyllyngys to teche hym that connynge / the
herde man after he had receyued his money sayde this. Spy se you not
yonder dun a kow with the whyte face/ yes quod the skoler. Suerly quod
ye herdma whe she dau syth and holdyth vp her tayle it shal haue a showre
of rayne within halfe an howre after.

By this ye may se ye the connyng of herdman & shepardes as touchyng
alteracyos of wedirs is more sure than ye indyvyallys of Astronomy.

IN a certayn town ther was a rych man that lay on his deth bed
at poynte of deth whiche chargyd his executours to dele for his
soule a certayn some of money in pence & on this condicyon char
gyd them as ye wolde answere afore. God that euery pore man that came
to them & tolde a trewe tale sholde haue a peny & they that sayd a fals thyn
ge sholde haue none/ & in the dole tyme there came one whiche sayd ye god
was a good man/quod ye executours thou shalt haue a peny for thou saydst
trouth. Anone came another & said ye deuyll was a good man quod the exe
cutours ther thou lyest therfore thou shalt haue nere a peny. At last came
one to ye executours & sayd this/ye shall gyue me nere a peny/which wor
dys made the executours amasyd and toke aduysement whether they shold
gyue hym the peny or no.

By this ye may se it is wysdome for Juggys in deutefull matters of
law to beware of hasty iugement.

A Man askyd his neybour which was but late maryed to a wydow
how he agreyd with his wyfe for he sayd ye her fyrst husbad and
she coud neuer agre by god quod ye other we agre meruelous wel
I pray ye how so/mary quod ye other I shall tell ye/when I am mery she is
mery/& when I am sad she is sad/for whe I goo out of my doris I am mery
to go from her & so is she/& when I come in agayne I am sad & so is she.

IN ye tyme of vysytacyo a byschop whiche was somwhat lecherous
& had got many chyldren preparyd to come to a prestes house to se
what rule he kept which prest had a lema in his house called Sede
by her had .ii. or .iii. smale chyldre in short space/but agayn ye bysshop com
mynge ye prest sparyd a rome to hyde his lema & his childre ouer in ye rofe of
his hall/& whe ye bysshop was come & set at dyner in ye same hal hauyng .r.
of his owne childre about hym this preste which coud speke lytell latyn or
none bad the bysshop in latyn to ete sayinge Comede episcope. This woma
in the rofe of the house herynge the prest say so bad wente he had callyd her

byddynge her com Edee & answerd shortly & sayd shall I brynge my chylde
ren wt me also. This bysshop herynge this word. tua sicut vitis abundans
in lateribus domus tue. The preest the half amasyd answeryd shortly and
sayd Filii tui sicut nouelle olyuarum in circuitu mense tue.

By this ye may se that they that haue but small lernynge somtyme spe
ke truely vnaduysyd.

ON asshe wednysday in ye mornynge was a curat of a chyrch whiche
had made good chere the nyght afore/& syttyn vp late & came to ye
chyrche to here confessyon to whom there came a woman/and amō
ge other thyngys she confessyd her that she had stolyn a pot. But than becau
se of grete watche that this preest had/he there sodenly felle a slepe/and
whē this woman sawe hym not wyllyng to here her she rose vp & wēt her
way/& anone an other woman kneled downe to the same prest & began to
say benedicite wherwith this preest sodenly wakyd wenynge she had ben
the other woma & sayd al angerly/what art thou now at benedicite agay
ne tell me what dydest thou when thou hadyst stolyn the pot.

SOne after one mayster whyttintō had byldED a colege on a nyght
as he slept he dremyd that he sad in his church & many folkys ther
also/& further he dremyd ye he sawe our lady in the same chyrch wt a glas
of goodly oyntement in her hand goynge to one askyng hym what he had
done for her sake/whiche sayd that he had sayd our ladys sauter euery day
wherfore she gaue hym a lytyll of the oyle. And anone se went to another
askyng hym what he had done for her sake which sayd that he had sayd.ii
ladys sauters euery day/wherfore our lady gaue hym more of ye oyntement
than she gaue ye other. This mayster whyttentō then thought that when
our ladydy sholde come to hym she wolde gyue hym all the hole glas bycause
ye he had byldED such a gret colege & was very glad in his mynd. But whē
our lady cam to hym she asked hym what he had suffred for her sake/which
wordys made hym gretly abasshyd bycause he had nothyng to say for hym
selfe/& so he dremyd that for all the gret dede of byldyng of ye sayd Colege
he had no parte of ye goodly oyntement.    By this ye may se that
to suffer for goddys sake is more meritoryous than to gyue gret goodys.

A Certayne bysshop appoynted to go on vysytacyon to a prestys hous
and bycause he wolde haue the preest do but lytell cost vpon hym he
bad hym dresse but lytyl mete sayng thus in latyn. Preparas mihi modicū
This prest which vnderstode hym not halfe wel had a horse callED modicū
wherfore he thought to obtayne the bysshops fauour & agaynst ye bysshops
comyng kplied his horse that was callED modicum wherof the byssop & his
seruātes ete yt which whē ye bisshop knew afterward was gretly displesid

    By this ye may se that many a fole doth moche cost which hath but
lytyll thank for his laboure.

A Certayne maltman of colbroke whiche was a very couetous wretche and had no pleasure but onely to get money came to London to fell his malt and broughte with hym .iiii. capons & there reseruyd .iiii. or .v. s. for malte and put it in a lytell purs tyed to his cote and after wente aboute the stretys to fell his capons whom a pollyng felowe that was a dycer and an vnthryft had espyed and Imagyned how he myght begyle the man other of his capons or of his money and came to this maltman in the strect berynge these capons in his hande and askyd hym how he wolde fell his capons and when he had shewyd hym the pryse of them he bad hym go with hym to his mayster and he wolde shew them to his mayster and he wolde cause hym to haue money for them wherto he agreed. This Poller wente to the cardynalls hat in lomberdys strete & when he came to the dore he toke the capons from the maltman and bad hym tary at the dore tyll he had shawed his mayster and he wolde come agayn to hym and brynge hym his money for them. This poller when he had goten the capons wente in to the house and wente thorowe the other bak entre in to Cornhyll and soo toke the capons with hym / and when this maltman had stond there a good season he askyd one of the tauerners where the man was that had the capons to shewe to his mayster / mary quod the tauerner I can not tell the here is nother mayster nor man in this house for this entre here is a comen hye way and gooth in to cornhyl I am sure he is gone aweye with thy capos. This maltman herynge that ran throwe the entre in to cornhyll and asayd for a felowe in a tawny cote that had capons in his hand. But no man coude tell hym whiche waye he was gone and soo the maltman loste his capons and after wente in to his Inne all heuy and sade and toke his horse to thentent to ryde home. This poller by that tyme had chaungyd his rapment and borowyd a furryd gowne and came to the maltman syttynge on horsback and sayd thus good man me thought I harde the inquire euyn now for one in a tawny cote that had stolyn from the .iiii. capos yf thou wylt gyue me a quart of wyne go with me and I shall brynge y to a place where he syttyth drynkyng with other felowes & had y capons in his hande. This maltman beynge glad therof grauntyd hym to gyue hym the wyne bycause he semyd to be an honest man / and went w hym vnto the dagger in chepe. This poller then sayd to hym go thy way streyght to thend of y long entre & there thou shalt se whether it be he or no & I wyl holde thy horse here tyll thou come agayn This maltman thynkyng to fynde the felow with his capos wet in & left his horse with the other at the dore. And as soone as he was gon in to the house this poller lad the horse awaye in to his owne lodgynge. This maltman inqueryd in the house for his felowe with the capons but no man

coulde tell hym no tydyngys of suche man /wherfore he canie agayne to þ
doze all sad ꝼ lokyd foz hym þ had his hozs to kepe/ ꝛ bycæuse he sawe hym
not he askyd dyuers there foz hym/ ꝛ some sayd they saw hym ꝛ some sayde
they saw hym not/but no man coude tell whiche waye he was gone wher
foze he wente home to his Inne moze sad thā he was befoze/wherfoze his
host gaue hym coūcell to get hym home ꝛ bewate how he trustyd any men
in londō. This maltman seynge none other cōfozt went his hy way home
watde. ¶ This poller which lyngeryd alway there aboute the Inne hard
tell that the maltman was goyng homewatde a fote apparelyd hym lyke
a mannys preutyse ꝛ gat a lytell boget stuffyd full of stones on his bake ꝛ
wente befoze hym to charynge crosse ꝛ taryed tyll þ maltman came/ꝛ as
kyd hym whether he wente whiche sayd to Colbroke. Mary quod þ other
I am glad therof foz I must goo to braynfozde to my mayster to bere hym
money which I haue in my boget ꝛ I wolde be glad of cōpany. This malt
man bycause of his owne money was glad of his cōpany/ꝛ so they agreed
ꝛ wente togyder a whyle. At the last this poller went somwhat befoze to
knyghtbrygge ꝛ sat vpon þ brydge ꝛ restyd hym with his boget on his bak/
ꝛ when he saw þ maltmā almost at hym he let his boget fall ouer þ brydge
in to þ water. ꝛ incontynent start vp ꝛ sayd to þ maltman alas I haue let
my boget fal in to þ water ꝛ there is .rl. ꝑi. of money therin/ yf thou wylt
wade in to þ water ꝛ go seke it ꝛ get it me agayne I shall gyue þ.rii. pence
foz thy labour/this maltman hauynge pyte of his losse ꝛ also glad to get
the .rii. pence plukyd of his hose cote ꝛ shyzt ꝛ wadyd into þ water to seke
foz the boget. And in þ mene whyle this poller gote his clothis ꝛ cote wher
to the purs of money was tyde ꝛ lepte ouer the hedge ꝛ wente to westmyn
ster. ¶ This maltman within a whyle after with grete payne ꝛ depe was
dynge founde þ boget ꝛ came out of the water ꝛ sawe not his felowe there
ꝛ sawe that his clothys ꝛ money were not there as he left them suspectyd þ
mater and openyd the boget and than founde nothynge therin but stonys
cryed out lyke a mad man and ran all nakyd to london agayne and sayde
alas alas helpe oz I shall be stolen. Foz my capons be stolen. My hozs is
stolen. My money and clothys be stolen and I shall be stolen myself. And
so ran aboute the stretys in london nakyd ꝛ mad cryenge alway I shall be
stole . I shall be stolen. And so contynuyd mad durynge his lyfe ꝛ so dyed
lyke a wzetche to the vtter dystruccyon of hymselfe ꝛ shame to all his kyn.

---

¶ By this ye may se that many a couetouse wzech þ louyd his good bet
ter than god and settyth his mynde inozdynatly theron by the ryghte
iugment of god oftymes comyth to a myserable and shamfull ende.

A Welcheman dwellynge in englonde foztuned to ſtele an englyſſ
mans cok ⁊ ſette it on ÿ fyze to ſeth wherfoze this englyſſ:man
ſuſpectyng ÿ welſſhmã cam in to his houſe ⁊ ſawe ÿ cok ſetyng on
ÿ fyze ⁊ ſayd to ÿ welchmã thus. Syz this is my cok. Mary qб ÿ welchinã
⁊ yf it be thyne ÿ ſhalt haue thy parte of it/nay quod ÿ englyſſ:nã ÿ is not
ynough. By cottes blut ⁊ her nayle quod ÿ welchmã yf her be not ynough
now her wyll be ynough anone foz her hath a good fyze vnder her.

Certayne of ÿ vycars of poulys dyſpoſyd to be mery on a ſondaye at
hye maſſe tyme ſent aɳother mad felowe of theyz accoyntaũce vnto
a folyſſhe dzonken pzeſte to gyue hym a botell/whiche man met with the
pzeſte vpon the top of ÿ ſtayzys by ÿ chaũcell doze ⁊ ſpake to hym ⁊ ſayde
thus. Syz my mayſter hath ſend you a botel to put your dzynke in bycauſe
ye can kepe none in your bzaynes. This pzeſte therwith beyng very angry
all ſodenly toke the botell ⁊ with his fote flange it downe in to ÿ body of
the chyzche vpon the gentylmens hedes:

A Certayne Iury in the counte of Myddelſex was inpaneld foz ÿ
kynge to inquere of all indytementes murders ⁊ felonyes. The
perſons of this panel were folyſſhe couetous ⁊ vnlerned/foz who
ſo euer wolde gyue thẽ a grote they wolde aſſyne ⁊ veryfy his byll whether
it were true oz fals ⱳout any other pzofe oz euidẽcc/wherfoze one ÿ was
a mery cõceytyd felowe perceyuyng theyz ſmale cõcyence ⁊ grete couetouſ:
nes put in a byll intytuled after this maner. Inquiratur pzo dño regi ſi Ie
ſus nazarenus furatus eſt vnũ aſinũ ad equitandum in egyptũ/⁊ gaue thẽ
a grote ⁊ deſyzed ÿ it myght be veryfyed. The ſayd Iury whiche loked all
on ÿ grote ⁊ nothyng on ÿ byll as was theyz vſe wzote billa vera on ÿ bak
therof which byll when it was pzeſentyd into ÿ court whẽ ÿ Iugys loked
theron they ſayd opẽly befoze all ÿ people lo ſyzs here is ÿ meruelouſt ver:
dyt ÿ euer was pzeſentyd by any inqueſt foz here they haue indyted Ieſu
of Nazareth foz ſtelyng of an aſſe which whẽ ÿ people hard it/it made thẽ
both to laugh ⁊ to wõder at ÿ folyſhnes ⁊ ſhãful piuri of the of ÿ equeſte.

By this ye may ſe it is grete parell to enpanell any iurrools vpon
any equeſt whiche be folyſſ ⁊ haue but ſmall conceyence.

In a certayn paryſſh a frere pzechyd/and in his ſermon he rebuked
them ÿ rode on ÿ ſonday/euer lokyng vpon one man ÿ was botyd
⁊ ſputtyd redy to ryde. This man perceyuyng ÿ all ÿ people notyd
hym ſodenly half in anger anſwerde ÿ frere thus /why pzechyſt ÿ ſo moch
agaynſt them ÿ ryde on ÿ ſonday foz cryſt hymſelfe dyde ryde on palme ſõ:
day/as thou knowyſt well it is wzyten in holy ſcrypture. To whõ ÿ frere
ſodẽly anſwerd ⁊ ſayd thus/but I pzay ÿ what cã therof was he not hãgid
on ÿ fryday after which heerynge all ÿ people in ÿ church fell on laughyng

There was a certayne man that had two sonnys vnlyke of condycy
ons. For the eldyst was lusty and qupk and vsyd moche to ryse erly
and walke in to the feldys/than was the yonger slowe and vnlusty and
vsyd to lye in bed as longe as he myght. So on a daye the elder as he was
wonte rose erly and walkyd in to the feldys and there by fortune he foun
de a purs of money and brought it home to his fader. His fader when
he had it wente streyght to his other sone yet lyenge then in his bed & sayd
to hym. O thou slogarde quod he seyst thou not thyne elder broder how he
by his erly rysyng had found a purs with money wherby we shalbe grete
ly holpen all oute lyfe/whyle thou sluggynge in thy bed dost no good but
slepe. He then wyst not what to sey but answeryd shortly and sayd fader
quod he yf he that hath lost the purs and money had lyne in his bed that sa
me tyme that he lost it as I do now my broder had founde no purs nor mo
ney to daye.

℣ By this ye may se that they that be accustompd in vyce and syn
wyl alway fynd one excuse or other to cloke there with theyr vyce
and vnthryftynes.

A Certayn wyfe there was whiche was somwhat fayre and as all
women be y be y fayre was somwhat proude of her bewty/& as
she and her mayd sat togeder she as one that was desyrous to be
preysyd sayd to her thus. I fayth Ione how tynkyst thou am I not a fayre
wyfe/yes by my trouth maystres quod she ye be the fayrest that euer was
except our lady/why by Cryst quod y maystres though our lady were good
yet she was not so fayre as men speke of.

℣ By this ye may se it is harde to fynde a bewtyouse woman with
out pryde.

A Certayne alderman of London there was lately dysceased whi
che now shall be nameles whiche was very couetouse as well
before he was maryed as after/for when he was bacheler euer
when his hosen were broken so that he coude were them no longer for
shame then wolde he cutte them of by the knee and putte on a payre of
ledder buskyns on his bare leggys whiche wolde laste hym a two or thre
yere. Furthermore it was his maner when he was a bacheler euery
nyght where that he was to borowe a candels ende to brynge hym home

whiche he wolde alway put in a chest that he had at his chamber. So that
by that tyme he was maryed / he had a cheste of candels endis that wayd
two or thre hondred weyghte. ¶ Sone after that he was maryed to a ryȝ
che wydowe and than folkys thought he wolde be better than he was before. But so it happenyd that a gentylman gaue hym a pasty of an harte
whiche euery day he caused to be sette on the table for seruyce / how beit he
wolde neuer for nygynshyp let it be openyd / so that it was a moneth or
bi. wekys or euer it was touched. It whiche tyme it fortuned a man of his
accoyntaunce beynge there often and seynge this pasty neuer to be openyd sayde syr by my trouth I wyll tame your pasty / whiche openyd ȳ pasty and incontynent lepte out. iii. or iiii. myce vpon other gentylmens trē
chowrs whiche had crept in at an hole vnderneche the bottam and hadde
etyn vp all the mete therin. Also this alderman was of suche condycyon ȳ
he wolde here. ii. or iii. masseys euery daye / and whan any pore folke came
to begge of hym he wolde rebuke them and say that they dyde lette hym in
heryng of them so that he wolde neuer gyue peny in almys. And on a tyme
as he sat at saynt Thomas of Acres herynge masse he sawe a yonge begyn
ner a dettour of his that owyd hym. xx. li. whiche as sone as he sawe hym
he commaunded one of his seruauntes to get a sergyaunt ȝ to arest hym
whiche yonge man immedyatly after was acestyd / and whan he was in
the counter he desyred dyuers of his frendys to intrete with this aldermā
for dayes of payment whiche men in the mornynge after came to this Alderman knelynge at masse ȝ intretyd hym for this man desyrynge hym to
take dayes of paymēt whiche answeryd them thus. I praye you troble me
not now for I haue harde one masse all redy ȝ I wyll here an other or I
medle with worldly matters. But yf ye haue the money here I wyll take
the now or elles I pray you speke to me no more / and so these men coude
get no other answer. And this Alderman kept this yonge man styll in pry
son tyll at the laste he there dyed. And so he causyd lykewyse dyuers other
to dye in pryson and wolde neuer forgyue them / wherfore afterward this
alderman dyed sodenly wherfore dyuers ȝ many were glad of his deth.


A Northen man there was whiche wente to seke hym a seruyce.
So it happenyd that he came to a lordys place whiche lord than
had war wȳ another lord. This lord thā askyd this northē mā yf
he durst fyght / ye by goddȳ bresȳ qȳ ȳ northē mā ȳ I dare for I is al hurt

wherbpon the lozde retayned hym in to his seruyce. So after it happenyd
ÿ this lozde sholde go fyght with his enmyes wᵗ whom also wēt this noz=
thēman which shortly was smytē in ÿ hele wᵗ an arow wherfoze he incō=
tynētly fell downe almost dede wherfoze one of his felaws sayd art thou
he ÿ art all hart and foz so lytyll a stroke in the hele now art almost dede.
To whom he answeryd ⁊ sayd by goddes sale I is hard hed/leggys/bodÿ
helps ⁊ all/therfoze ought not one to fere when he is stryken in ÿ hart.

In a certayn towne there was a wyfe somwhat agyd that had be=
ryed her husband whose name was callyd John/whom she loued
so tenderly in his lyfe that after his deth she cauſyd an ymage of
tymber to be made in vysage and person as lyᵏ e to hym as coulde be/whi=
che pmage all day longe lay vnder her bed and euery nygh⁺ she cauſyd her
mayde to wzap it in a shete ⁊ lay it in her bed ⁊ callyd it olde John . This
wyfe also had a pzety se whose name was John/which John wolde fayn
haue weddyd his maystres not foz no grete pleaſur but onely foz her good
bycauſe she was rych/wherfoz he imagynyd how he might obtayn his pur
poſe ⁊ spake to ÿ mayde of ÿ hous ⁊ deſyzyd her to lay hym in his maystres
bed foz one nyght in stede of the pycture/⁊ pzomyſed her a rewarde foz her
laboure/which mayd ouer nyght wzapppd ÿ ſayd yōg mā in a shete ⁊ layd
hym in his maystres bed as she was wōt to lay ÿ pycture. ¶ This wydow
was wont euery nyght befoze she slept ⁊ dyuers tymes whē she wakyd to
kys the ſayd pycture of old John/wherfoze ÿ ſayd nyght she kyſſyd ÿ ſayd
yong mā beleuyng that she had kyſt ÿ pycture/⁊ he ſodēly start ⁊ toke her
in his armys and so well pleſed her then/that olde John from thēs fozth
was clene out of her mynde ⁊ was cōtent ÿ this yonge John sholde lye wᵗ
her styl all ÿ nyght ⁊ ÿ the pycture of olde John sholde lye styl vnder ÿ bed
foz a thyng of nought. After this in ÿ moznynge this wydow intendyng
to pleſe this yōg John which had made her ſo good paſtyme all the nyght
bad her mayd go dzeſſe ſome good mete foz theyz bzekefaſt to fell therwith
her yōg John. this mayd whā she had lōge ſought foz wood to dzeſ ÿ layd
mete told her maſtres ÿ she coud fynd no wood ÿ was dzy except onely ÿ pic
ture of old John ÿ lyeth vnder ÿ bed/thē qd ÿ wyf agayn/fat h hym down
⁊ lay hym on ÿ fyze foz I ſe well he wyll neuer do me good noz he wyl ne
uer do better ſeruyce though I kepe hym neuer ſo longe. So the mayd by
her cōmaundemēt fet the pycture of old John frō vnder ÿ bed ⁊ therwith
made good fyze ⁊ dzeſſid ÿ bzekfaſt/⁊ ſo olde John was caſt out foz nought
⁊ ozent ⁊ frōm thens fozth yong John occupyed his place.

¶ By this tale ye may ſe it is no wyſdome foz a mā to kepe longe oz to
chyzyſhe that thyng ÿ is able to do no pleaſure noz ſeruyce.
¶ Finis.

¶This endeth the booke of a. C. mery
talys. Emprynted at London at the sygne of
the Merymayd At Powlys gate next
to chepe syde. ¶The yere
of our Lorde. M: v. C.
xxvi. ¶The xxii.
day of Nouēber.

Johannes · Rastell

¶Cum preuilegio
Regali.

www.ingramcontent.com/pod-product-compliance
Lightning Source LLC
Chambersburg PA
CBHW031446270326
41930CB00007B/886